Scottish
Proverbs

Scottish Proverbs

COLIN S. K. WALKER

BIRLINN

This edition published in 2021 by
Birlinn Limited
West Newington House
10 Newington Road
Edinburgh
EH9 1QS

www.birlinn.co.uk

First published in 1996

ISBN 978 1 78027 729 5

Designed and typeset by Mark Blackadder

Printed and bound by MBM Print SCS Ltd, Glasgow

Introduction

The definition of a proverb is no simple matter and has occupied scholars from Ancient Greece until the present day. Lord John Russell defined the proverb as 'the wisdom of many and the wit of one'. The celebrated Spanish writer Cervantes said that a proverb is 'a short sentence drawn from long experience'. Generally it is accepted that a proverb is a short, pithy traditional saying, which contains some widely accepted knowledge, or which offers advice or presents a moral. This present volume also contains many phrases and sayings which are not strictly proverbs as we use the term today, although we may still think of them as such. This situation arises because, prior to the eighteenth century it was common for the term to include metaphors, similes, and descriptive epithets. I have included these 'rogue' phrases or sayings, as much for the continuance of the tradition established by previous collectors, as from the difficulty of finding any easy rule by which to distinguish them. The essence of a proverb lies in it being a 'traditional saying' i.e. something which has commonly passed from one generation to another by word of mouth. Hence it would not seem appropriate to reject any of these 'rogue' sayings as their usage embraces much that is essential to the true proverb. In his book *On the Lessons in Proverbs* (1852), Richard Chevenix Trenchard says that there is one quality of the proverb which is the most essential of all:

> … popularity, acceptance and adoption on the part of the people. Without this popularity, without these suffrages and this consent of the many, no saying, however seasoned with salt, however worthy on all

these accounts to have become a proverb, however fulfilling all other its conditions, can yet be esteemed as such.

What is the importance of proverbs to Scottish culture and heritage? Proverbs can provide us not only with the wisdom gathered by our forebears but also with a unique insight into the way of life or social mores of past generations. Many of the proverbs contained in this book date from a pre-industrial Scotland, when the majority of people still lived off the land or sea, and hence contain the rich vocabulary associated with these disappearing or extinct lifestyles. A strong impression is created of a society in which hard work was necessary merely to subsist, and the Scottish Protestant work ethic is well to the fore in many of the sayings. Although we would no longer consider them to be 'politically correct', there are a considerable number of proverbs relating to marriage guidance, or giving advice to men on how to deal with women. From these sayings we can trace the changes which have taken place in our society. As the poet William Motherwell put it, in his eloquent introduction to Henderson's book of *Scottish Proverbs* in 1832:

> The study of proverbs may be more instructive and comprehensive than the most elaborated scheme of philosophy; and in relation to changes in the manners of people, their customs, and various minute incidents connected either with places or persons, they often preserve particulars which contemporary history has failed to record.

For any true student of Scottish culture, the proverb has a twofold reason for being studied: (1) for its own intrinsic worth, and (2) for its associations with the wisdom of past generations of the race.

In many ways, a book of proverbs can be said to contain the philosophy of the common people, or a nation's distilled wisdom. (The latter phrase would seem particularly appropriate when one counts the number of Scottish proverbs relating to drink!)

Perhaps the strongest thread running through most of the proverbs contained in this book relates to the Scottish nation's pawky sense of humour. For a language such as Scots, with its rich oral tradition, it is essential that we not only conserve the proverbs of the past, but also record new ones which reflect the times and places in which we now live. Proverbs are an essential part of our living culture and heritage, and should be valued as such. In his book *A Complete Collection of Scottish Proverbs* (1721) James Kelly bears testimony to the widespread use of proverbs at that time. He says that: 'there were current in society upwards of 3,000 proverbs, exclusively Scottish.'

He adds:

> The Scots are wonderfully given to this way of speaking and, as the consequence of that, abound with proverbs, many of which are very expressive, quick, and home to the purpose; and, indeed, this humor prevails among the better sort of the commonalty, none of whom will discourse with you any considerable time, but he will affirm every assertion and observation with a Scottish Proverb.

From this statement we can see what a massive sea-change has taken place in society as regards the 'proverbial' mode of intercourse. In Kelly's day it was common practice in conversation to strengthen an argument or illustrate a point by using a proverb. According to Lord Bacon, proverbs:

> serve not only for ornament and delight, but also for active and civil use; as being the edge tools of speech which cut and penetrate the knots of business and affairs.

Proverbs can be seen in some ways as the germ of moral and political science. However, they are the product of the common people, and do not owe their origins to the ivory towers of academia or to baronial mansions. For this reason the use of proverbs was considered vulgar by later generations of educated Scots, and their formal application was almost prohibited by the rules of polite society. The coming of a more educated and industrialised society also brought about a change in the method of communication. Oral transmission of a society's knowledge ceased to be the preferred method of communication and was instead replaced by the written and printed word.

I am greatly indebted to the works of the great Scottish proverb documentors of the sixteenth, seventeenth, eighteenth and nineteenth centuries (Fergusson, Henderson, Hislop, Kelly, and Ramsay) for many of the older proverbs.

It seems like poetic justice that Fife (proverbially known as the Kingdom of Fife, though it never had a King) can claim to be the home of the first written collection of Scottish proverbs. It was made by David Ferguson, a minister from Dunfermline in the latter half of the sixteenth century, put *ordine alphabetico* when he died in 1598, but not published until 1641. His collection by the time of his death amounted to 945 sayings, and were given without any comment or explanation. They were printed in Edinburgh without an author's preface but instead with an address from the printer in which he said:

> … I know that there may be some that will say and marvell that a minister should have taken pains to gather such proverbs together; but they that knew his forme of powerfull preaching the word, and his ordinar talking, ever almost using proverbiall speeches will not finde fault with this that he hath done.

This first collection was later published together with a larger manuscript collection of about the same period in Edinburgh in 1924 under the editorship of E. Beveridge.

In 1721 *A Complete Collection of Scottish Proverbs Explained and made Intelligible to the English Reader*, by James Kelly M.A. was published in London. It contains a short explanation or commentary attached to each proverb, along with some parallel sayings from other languages. In his introduction Kelly describes his own disappointment at making the discovery that for many of the proverbs it is difficult to distinguish their nation of origin. He also says that he has 'omitted in his collection many popular proverbs which are very pat and expressive', giving the reason that 'since it does not become a man of manners to use them it does not become a man of my age and profession to write them'.

Allan Ramsay the famous poet published *A Collection of Scots Proverbs* dedicated to the tenantry of Scotland in 1737, bearing the appropriate motto on the title page: 'That maun be true that a' men say'. Unlike Kelly's collection which was written for the English reader, Ramsay's collection is very Scottish in its style, not only with the proverbs themselves, but also his dedication to the tenantry of Scotland, prefixed to the collection, which is written in pure Scots dialect. In this dedication he says:

> As naething helps our happiness mair than to have the mind made up wi' right principles, I desire you, for the thriving and pleasure of you and yours, to use your een and lend your lugs to these guid auld saws, that shine wi' wail'd sense, and will as lang as the world wags.

This edition of Ramsay's collection contains a total of 2,464 proverbs, and professes to correct the errors of former collectors.

Andrew Henderson published his collection *Scottish Proverbs*, with an excellent introductory essay by his life-long friend the poet William Motherwell, in Edinburgh in 1832. This collection was largely a compilation from previous printed collections as later was Alexander Hislop's *The Proverbs of Scotland* (1862), to which he made large additions from the works of Sir Walter Scott, Gait, Hogg, and other national writers.

This present collection is but a selection of the more widely known and used Scottish proverbs and sayings, drawing heavily upon the excellent work of these earlier collectors.

I have arranged the dictionary in an easily accessible alphabetical format, according to the first word of each proverb. In the past, some scholars have attempted to arrange proverbs according to their subjects, but this has never proved to be entirely satisfactory, because many proverbs prove too difficult to classify. For example, in Hislop's collection, the second part of the book contains the proverbs classified by subject, of which there are 148. He says of his classification that it:

> has been a work of very great labour, and, indeed attended with most unsatisfactory results. The difficulty of reducing a great number of proverbs, of almost universal application, into distinct, individual subjects can only be understood by those who have attempted the operation; while the greater number, which absolutely defy classification, add greatly to the difficulties of the task.

Most of the proverbs are listed with an attendant note or explanation of their meaning. I will apologise in advance for the inadequacies of my explanations; it is not always possible to provide accurate and succinct alternatives for finely tuned phrases of 'distilled wisdom'. I merely hope that they may be of occasional use to the reader.

It is never easy to prove that any proverb or saying belongs to one particular country, or district, unless it contains a place-name or some distinctive feature. Even then a true proverb is never parochial, its true meaning has no boundaries. Nations are constantly borrowing proverbs from each other. The original stock of proverbs with which a nation starts are either orally handed down to it, or made part of its own stock by those early writers who brought it into living communication with the past. Hence the common traditions of the civilised world have been preserved and passed down, ensuring that many Greek, Latin, and medieval proverbs are kept alive in many modern nations of the world. I have carefully selected those proverbs which I believe contain some truly Scottish essence. Some, but not all, of the proverbs are exclusively Scottish – some are common to several different countries. Nevertheless, the language used gives them a peculiarly Scottish slant, or way of looking at the world, and I have included them for this reason.

At the end of the book I have provided a simple glossary of the Scots words used, to act as an aid for those unfamiliar with the language.

I sincerely hope that you will enjoy meeting some old familiar friends in this volume, as well as discovering some new ones.

Colin S.K. Walker, 1996

A' ae oo.
It's all for a common end. The above saying is a
demonstration of the peculiarly powerful use of vowels in the
Scottish dialect. An anecdote is recorded of the conversation
between a shopkeeper and a customer relating to a plaid
hanging at the shop door.
Cust: (Inquiring of the material) Oo? (Wool?)
Shop: Aye oo (Yes, it's made of wool)
Cust: A' oo? (All wool?)
Shop: Aye, a' oo (Yes, all wool)
Cust: A' ae oo? (All the same wool?)
Shop: Aye a' ae oo (Yes, all the same wool).

**A' are good lasses, but where do the ill wives come
frae?**
A suggestion that marriage changes some women.

A' are no friends that speak us fair.
You cannot trust to the friendship of everyone who pays you
a compliment.

A bad wound may heal, but a bad name will kill.
It is possible to recover from physical injury, but not if injury
has been caused to one's reputation.

A bairn maun creep afore it gangs.
A learner must master the basics, before trying something
more difficult. Perfection is only to be attained through
practice.

A bald heid is soon shaven.
A slight task is soon completed.

A bawbee cat may look at a King.

A beggar's wallet is a mile to the bottom.
This is because it generally contrives to contain all he gets.

'A begun turn is half ended', quo' the wife when she stuck the graip in the midden.
Half the battle with work is getting it started.

A bird in the hand's worth twa fleeing bye, or in the bush.
A small certainty is of more use than a larger uncertainty.

A bit but and a bit ben maks a mim maiden at the board end.
A joke aimed at women who eat little at the dinner table, suggesting that they would have a keener appetite if they had not already sampled the food in the kitchen.

A bit is often better gi'en than eaten.
On certain occasions it is better to give than receive.

A blate cat maks a proud mouse.
When those who are in charge are not very forceful, those they are supposed to be leading are apt to take advantage.

A blind man has nae need o' a looking-glass.

A blind man's wife needs nae painting.

A body's no broke while they hae a gude kail stock.
When all is not lost, it is still possible that all may be saved.

A bold foe is better than a cowardly friend.
At least you can judge how the former will behave in a given situation.

A bonny bride is soon buskit, and a short horse soon wispit.
A good-looking bride needs little in the way of adornment, and a small horse is soon groomed, i.e. a slight task is soon finished.

A bonny gryce may mak an ugly old sow.
A warning to young girls that their beauty may not last with age.

A borrowed len' should gae laughing hame.
A cautionary note to look after borrowed goods and to return them in good condition and with a good grace.

About the moon there is a brugh; the weather will be cold and rough.
A weather warning if you see a halo effect around the moon.

A broken kebbuck gangs sune dune.
Once started, food does not last long.

Abundance o' law breaks nae law.
It is less likely that people who know the law will break it than those who are ignorant of it.

A cauld needs the cook as muckle as the doctor.
Many say the best remedy for a cold is to feed it.

'A clean thing's kindly,' quo' the wife when she turned her sark after a month's wear.

A close mouth catches nae flees.
The person who keeps their mouth shut will also keep out of trouble.

A cock's aye crouse on his ain midden head.
It's much easier for people to be courageous on their own territory.

A covetous man is gude to nane, but warst to himsel.
Avarice does nobody any good, least of all the person who feels it.

A coward's fear maks a brave man braver.

A crackit bell will never mend.
It is pointless wasting effort trying to mend things which are irretrievably damaged.

A crammed kyte maks a crazy carcase.
A man is more likely to enjoy himself on a full stomach than on an empty one.

A craw is nae whiter for being washed.
The Scottish equivalent of the leopard and his spots.

A Crook in the Forth;
Is worth an Earldom in the North.
When it reaches the low carse lands near Stirling, the River Forth pursues a very meandering course giving rise to many 'crooks' or bends. This land is very fertile, hence owning a small piece of it will bring in an equivalent income to owning a large estate in the highlands.

A crooning coo, a crawing hen, and a whistlin' maid were ne'er very chancy.
To make sure their behaviour was seemly, young girls were told that these three things were unnatural, and hence to be avoided.

A day to come seems langer than a year that's gane.
Waiting for something in the future seems to take forever.

A deaf man will hear the clink o' money.

A dink maiden oft maks a dirty wife.
Some neat maidens forget their neat habits when they get married.

A dish o' married love right sune grows cauld, and dosens down to nane as folk grow auld.
An early piece of unsentimental Scottish marriage guidance.

A dog winna yowl if ye fell him wi' a bane.
You will not hurt a dog by throwing bones at him.

A doucer man ne'er broke warld's bread.
A saying expressive of unqualified respect.

A drap and a bite's but a sma' requite.
A request to friends to have some food and drink, which is but small recompense for their friendship.

A dreigh drink is better than a dry sermon.
The first you can leave if it is not to your taste, the second you have to endure.

A drink is shorter than a tale.
An excuse given by some for drinking during the telling of a tale.

A dry summer ne'er made a dear peck.

A dumb man hauds a'.
i.e. A dumb man cannot disclose anything.

A dumb man wins nae law.
A talkative advocate is more likely to win his case than a taciturn one.

Ae half o' the world disna ken how the ither half lives.
Sadly one wonders sometimes if they even care, let alone know.

Ae man may steal a horse where anither daurna look ower the hedge.
This saying is used to demonstrate the value of having a good name and reputation. A man with a blameless character can get away with murder, whereas an individual with a poor reputation will always be suspected of being up to no good.

Ae scabbit sheep will smit a hail hirsel.
It only takes one rotten apple to spoil the barrel.

Ae shook o' that stook's enough.
One is enough as a sample.

A fair maid tocherless will get mair wooers than husbands.
A sceptic's view that a Scotsman's wallet is more powerful than his heart.

Affront your friend in daffin', and tine him in earnest.
Do not offend a friend even in jest or you may lose him for good.

A fleyer would aye hae a follower.
A coward, or someone who does wrong, generally likes to involve another person in their actions.

A fool is happier thinking weel o' himsel than a wise man is of ithers thinking weel o' him.
A caution to the self obsessed.

A fool may gie a wise man counsel.

A fool's bolt is soon shot.
Some people lacking in wisdom do not hesitate to give their opinions on important matters without giving them serious consideration first.

A friend's dinner is soon dished.
A true friend can be treated like a member of the family, is easily served, and will not readily take offence.

Aft counting keeps friends lang thegither.
People with short accounts make long friendships with each other.

After dinner sit a while, after supper walk a mile.

After words come weird: fair fa' them that ca's me Madam.
Roughly this means that after libel comes proof – let them that speak ill of me look to themselves.

Aft ettle, whiles hit.
Try often, occasionally succeed.

A fu' heart never lied.
The truth generally comes out when a person is governed by their feelings.

A fu' purse maks a haverin' merchant.
A man with a full purse who is engaged in a commercial transaction is likely to haver, or gossip, because he does not feel financially compelled to urgently conclude the deal.

A fu' sack can bear a clout i' the side.
A well-to-do person can afford to take a few knocks from those less fortunate.

A fu' wame maks a straight back.
A proverb of similar sentiment to the last one.

A gaun fit's aye getting, were it but a thorn or a broken tae.
An industrious person will always be rewarded for their efforts, but the proverb warns that it might not be what the person desires.

A gi'en game was ne'er won.
A conceded game may be of no tribute to the skill of the
opponent.

A gi'en piece is soon eaten.
A small favour is soon forgotten.

A gowk at Yule'll no be bright at Beltane.
Literally this means that the person who is a fool at
Christmas will not be wise in May. i.e You cannot change a
person's inherited character.

A greedy ee ne'er got a fu' wame.
A warning that the greedy are never satisfied.

A green turf is a gude gudemother.
An old mother-in-law joke, i.e. the best place for her is in the
churchyard.

A green Yule and a white Pasch mak a fat kirkyard.
A rather unfeeling proverb, reflecting the effects of the
seasons on the frail human frame.

**A grunting horse and a graneing wife seldom fail their
master.**
A case of the 'Creaking gate' syndrome. Those who
constantly complain that they are on their last legs, often
contrive to live as long as their neighbours.

A gude calf is better than a calf o' a good kind.
The former is good already whereas the latter might possibly
turn out bad.

**A gude face needs nae band, and an ill face deserves
nane.**
An honest face needs no recommendation and a dishonest
one does not deserve one.

A gude fellow ne'er tint but at an ill fellow's hand.
Only a dishonest person would cheat another person.

A gude name is sooner tint than won.
It only takes one bad act to ruin a reputation.

A gude tale is no' the waur o' bein' twice tauld.

A gude year winna mak him, nor an ill year mar him.
The person thus addressed is already comfortably off.

A hairy man's a geary man, but a hairy wife's a witch.
In the sixteenth and seventeenth centuries it was the fashion for successful and wealthy men to wear beards. This was also the era for witch hunting.

A handfu' o' trade is worth a gowpen o' gold.
A little knowledge of a trade will pay dividends in the end.

A hantle cry Murder! and are aye upmost.
It is often the case that those who are least hurt cry the loudest.

A hook is weel tint to catch a salmon.
It generally pays off if one is prepared to lose a little in order to win a lot.

A horn spoon holds nae poison.
It is generally safe to eat at a humble table, because they do not attract poisoners.

A horse hired never tired.
This saying alludes to the fact that many people tend to look after their own possessions better than those which they may have hired or borrowed.

A houndless hunter and a gunless gunner see aye routh o' game.
You only see what you want when you can't have it.

A house fu' o' folk and a pouch wi' three fardens i' the corner o't dinna sort weel thegither.
Poverty and a desire to keep up appearances in front of others is an uneasy combination.

A hungry man's an angry man.
This saying was first recorded in Fergusson's *Scottish Proverbs* (1641) as "Hungry men ar angry".

A hungry man's meat is lang o' makin' ready.
The watched pot never boils, or at least never seems to.

A hungry wame has nae lugs.
Those who are hungry are deaf to reason.

A kiss and a drink o' water mak but a wersh breakfast.
A warning to those who might marry for love without thought of their future means.

A layin' hen is better than a standin' mill.
The first may be small but it at least makes a profit, whereas the latter does not.

Ale-sellers shouldna be tale-tellers.
It is expected that publicans will listen but not repeat all that they hear, and it is prudent that they do so if they wish to keep their customers.

A light-heeled mother maks a heavy-heeled dochter.
An active and industrious mother can sometimes do too much work around the home and hence leave little for the daughter to do so that she grows up being less industrious. This saying obviously predates any thoughts of equal opportunities for the sexes.

A' cracks maunna be trew'd.
You shouldn't believe all that you hear.

All craiks, all bears.
Spoken against people who complain about everything but
do nothing to change their situation.

A' his buz shakes nae barley.
All his talking changes nothing.

**A' I got frae him I could put i' my e'e, and see nane the
waur for it.**
A saying used by a person who feels that they have not
received a just reward for their efforts for another.

**A's no gowd that glisters, nor maidens that wear their
hair.**
Not everything is as it first appears. In eighteenth-century
Scotland it was the fashion for virgins to go bareheaded. The
speaker of this proverb is questioning the honesty of some of
the women not wearing headdresses.

A's tint that's put in a riven dish.
Favours bestowed upon unworthy recipients are wasted.

A' Stuarts are no sib to the King.
People may have the name and appearance of greatness
without the reality.

A' the keys of the country hang na in ae belt.
All the power is not in one person's possession.

A' to ae side, like Gourock.
Said when something is squint.

A man canna bear a' his kin about on his back.
No man can be expected to support all of his relations.

A man canna wive and thrive in the same year.
An unsentimental comment upon the cost of marriage.

A man may spit in his neive and do but little.
A person may make a great show of their intentions to work, but actually do very little.

A man may woo where he will, but maun wed where his weird is.
A suggestion that marriage partners are already decided by fate.

A man o' words, but no o' deeds, is like a garden fu' o' weeds.

A man's a man for a' that.
The refrain from Robert Burns' song of brotherhood.

A mile o' Don's worth twa o' Dee; Except for salmon, stane and tree.
An Aberdeenshire saying expressing the differences in the value of the terrain surrounding the two rivers. The banks of the Don are very fertile, whereas Deeside tends to be more wilderness and forest.

A mouthfu' o' meat may be a tounfu' o' shame.
That is, if a small thing has been procured by foul means, it may bring great disgrace upon the offender.

An auld pock needs muckle clouting.
Old things generally are often in need of repair.

An auld tout on a new horn is little minded.
An old story or complaint will receive little attention, even if it is told in a different way, or by a different person.

Ance awa, aye awa.
Once a person has gone away from home for a while, there is always a feeling that it will not take too much to persuade them to leave again.

Ance provost, aye My Lord.
Once a person has been Provost they get to keep their title even when they have left office. Hence this proverb suggests that once a good or bad name has been attached to someone, it is very difficult to get rid of thereafter.

An elbuck dirl will lang play thirl.
'An elbuck dirl' is a knock or blow to one's elbow which has a very stunning effect for a time, i.e. a particular cause will have a particular effect.

Ane may like the kirk weel enough, and no ride on the riggin' o't.
A jibe at fanatics. One can be keen on something without taking it to extremes.

Ane o' the court, but nane o' the council.
Although the person thus addressed may be asked for their opinion, it is only for form's sake.

A new pair o' breeks will cast down an old coat.
Literally this means that wearing a new item of clothing will only serve to make the other items look old and shabby. This saying was sometimes used when an old man married a young girl.

An ilka-day braw maks a Sabbath-day daw.
A person who wears their best outfit everyday, will have nothing suitable for special occasions.

An ill cow may hae a gude calf.
Bad parents may produce good children.

An ill custom is like a gude bannock – better broken than kept.

An ill shearer ne'er got a gude heuk.
It is a poor workman who blames his tools.

An olite mither maks a sweird dochter.
A mother who is over industrious is apt to leave little for her offspring to do, leading them to grow up lazy.

An ounce o' wit is worth a pound o' lear.
An ounce of natural wit is worth a pound of wit learnt at school.

A proud mind and a poor purse gree ill thegither.

A raggit cowte may prove a gude gelding.
An unpromising colt may turn out to be a fine horse, i.e. one cannot always tell how something will develop in the future.

As ane flits anither fits, and that keeps mailins dear.
The law of supply and demand tends to keep prices (or in this case farms) relatively stable, i.e. they don't get any cheaper.

As auld as the Moss o' Meigle.
Said of very old things.

A scar'd head is soon broken.
It does not take much to completely ruin the name of someone whose reputation has already been called into question before.

A Scots mist will weet an Englishman to the skin.
A proverb arising from the frequent complaints of English visitors of the heavy mists which hang about the Highlands of Scotland.

A Scotsman and a Newcastle grindstane travel a' the world ower.
Both these things are known for their fine qualities, and hence are welcomed throughout the world.

A Scotsman is aye wise ahint the hand.

As gude eat the deil as sup the kail he's boil'd in.
It is as well to do something (perhaps commit a sin) in an
obvious manner as to try to achieve the same results by
stealth.

As gude may haud the stirrup as he that loups on.
One cannot judge a man merely by his position in life.

A sillerless man gangs fast throught the market.
Because he doesn't have the necessary money with which to
buy or bargain.

As menseless as a tinkler's messan.
As ill-bred as a tinker's dog.

A sooth bourd's nae bourd.
A true jest is no jest at all.

As slow's the Tweed at Muir House.
A saying local to Melrose, evidently used in a sarcastic sense
because the river runs swiftly at this point.

As sure's death.
A common expression signifying either the truth or certainty
of a fact, or to pledge the speaker to a performance of his
promise. In the Eglinton Papers the Earl gives an amusing
anecdote illustrating this latter sense of the phrase. One day
the Earl found a boy climbing up a tree, and called him to
come down. The boy declined, because, he said, the earl
would thrash him. His lordship pledged his honour that he
would not do so. The boy replied, 'I dinna ken onything
about your honour, but if you say as sure's death I'll come
down.'

As the auld cock craws, the young ane learns.
A proverb denoting the legacy of learnt behaviour.

As the day lengthens the cold strengthens.
A proverbial weather warning. As the days start to get longer in February and March, the weather can be even colder than in December or January.

As the wind blaws seek your beild.
Suit your way of life to your circumstances.

As tired as a tyke is o' langkail.
Literally, as tired as a dog is of the same kind of meat every day.

As weel be sune as syne.
A saying used to suggest that a thing is as well done now rather than put off until later.

As wight as a wabster's doublet, that ilka day taks a thief by the neck.
An allegation that the weaving fraternity tended to be dishonest. For some unknown reason this particular trade comes in for a lot of abuse in proverbs.

A tocher's nae word in a true lover's parle.
True love is not mercenary – money is of no consequence.

A toom pantry maks a thriftless gudewife.
When the cupboard is bare, there is nothing for the housewife to be thrifty with.

Auld men are twice bairns.
A saying suggesting that old men behave like they did when they were young children.

Auld sparrows are ill tae tame.
Another version of trying to teach an old dog new tricks, i.e. the older one gets, the more set in one's ways one becomes.

Auld wives and bairns mak fools o' physicians.
The elderly can do so by virtue of experience, and children through ignorance.

A wee bush is better than nae beild.
A small shelter is better than nothing.

A wee house has a wide mouth.
A warning that no matter how small a household is, it still takes more than one thinks to support it.

A wise man carries his cloak in fair weather, an' a fool wants his in rain.
A word of encouragement to the cautious. Be prepared.

A wise man gets learning frae them that hae nane o' their ane.
A clever person can learn from the mistakes of others.

A yeld sow was never glide to gryces.
A proverbial expression insinuating that those who are childless are rarely good with the children of others.

Aye to eild, but never to wit.
A description of someone who continues to grow older, but no wiser.

A Yule feast may be done at Pasch.
Festivities although normally practised at Christmas need not be confined to any particular season if a suitable occasion demands.

Bachelors' wives and auld maids' bairns are aye weel bred.
A reply to those who give advice on matters of which they have no personal experience.

Bad legs and ill wives should aye stay at home.

Bairns are certain care, but nae sure joy.
A warning of the realities of parenthood.

Bairns speak i' the field what they hear i' the ha'.
A warning to all parents to be mindful what they say in earshot of children.

Bannocks are better than nae bread.
Half a loaf is better than no bread at all.

Barefooted folk shouldna tread on thorns.
Another version of the English 'Those who live in glass houses should not throw stones'.

Beauty's muck when honour's tint.
Beauty no longer has any worth when honour is lost.

Be aye the thing ye would be ca'd.
Always try to live up to the standards you would want to be known by.

'Because' is a woman's reason.

Beds are best, quo' the man to his guest.
This saying was presumably used in the interests of
economy, i.e. the host wanted his guest to go straight to bed
and hence would avoid having to supply him with any
supper.

**Bees that hae honey in their mouths hae stings in their
tails.**
A warning to be wary of silver-tongued individuals who are
often up to no good.

Before I ween'd: but now, I wat.
This phrase is spoken when we finally find evidence of some
wrongdoing of which we could only suspect beforehand, i.e.
before I suspected, now I know for certain.

Before the deil gaes blind, and he's no blear e'ed yet.
A reply informing the questioner that what they request will
be at some time in the future – if at all.

Beggars shouldna be choosers.

**Begin wi' needles and preens, and end wi' horn'd
nowte.**
Small beginnings can often lead onto much greater things.
The saying is used here as a warning against dishonesty.

Be it sae, is nae banning.
Spoken when yielding a point in an argument because you
are either unwilling or unable to go further, but also
indicating that you still think yourself to be in the right.

Belyve is twa hours and a half.
The person who says that they will do something
immediately, or shortly, will probably take longer than
anticipated.

Be ready wi' your bannet, but slow wi' your purse.
A suggestion that if you are busy raising your hat to be polite you may get out of dipping your hand into your purse to pay for things.

Best to be off wi' the auld love before we be on wi' the new.
A warning of the dangers of two-timing.

Be thou weal, or be thou wae, thou wilt not aye be sae.
One cannot always predict what one's circumstances will be in the future.

Better a clout in than a hole out.
An item of clothing with a patch is preferable to one full of holes.

Better a finger aff than aye waggin'.
It is better to face the worst than to always have some evil hanging over you.

Better a fremit friend than a friend fremit.
Better a strange friend than a friend turned stranger.

Better an auld man's darling than a young man's warling.
A saying sometimes used to induce young girls to marry an older man.

Better a tocher in her than wi' her.
Better the woman with good qualities and no money than vice versa.

Better a wee bush than nae beild.
Better to have something, no matter how small, than nothing at all.

Better bairns greet than bearded men.
This saying was commonly used in the past to justify strict
measures, especially when punishment was being handed
out to children. According to one story John Knox used an
amended form of this proverb when he made Mary Queen of
Scots cry in his attempts to convert her to Protestantism. He
substituted the word 'women' for 'bairns'.

Better belly burst than gude meat spoil.
A saying used by gluttons to justify their greed, on the
grounds of economy.

Better be sonsy than soon up.
It's better to be naturally fortunate than to have to get up
early to make one's fortune.

Better gang about than fa' in the dub.
It is sometimes safer to take the long way round than to try
the shortcut.

Better greet ower your gudes than after your gudes.
It is better not to sell your wares than to sell them and not
receive any payment.

Better hain weel than work fair.
It is better to economise than to toil for a greater subsistence.

Better haud out than put out.
Prevention is better than cure.

**Better learn frae your neebor's skaith than frae your
ain.**
It is better to learn from others' mistakes than from your
own.

Better leave than lack.
It is better to have too much than too little of some things.

Better mak your feet your friends.
Said as a warning, meaning run for your life!

Better my friends think me fremit than fashious.
It is better to visit friends seldom than to be such a constant caller that you become a nuisance.

Better ower't than on't.
It is better to be beyond the fear of danger than in it.

Better rough an' sonsy than bare an' donsy.
It is better to be a fortunate rough diamond than to be an unlucky person from a genteel background.

Better rue sit than rue flit.
It is better not to remove house at all than to move and then regret it.

Better saucht wi' little aucht than care wi' mony cows.
It is better to have little and peace of mind than to have a lot and all its worries.

Better skaiths saved than mends made.
It is better not to offend to begin with than to have to apologise later.

Better thole a grumph than a sumph.
It is preferable to be troubled by an intelligent, though surly man, than by a stupid one.

Better to wed ower the midden than ower the moor.
It is better to marry a neighbour than a stranger. This proverb predates 1628 as it is recorded in M.L. Anderson's *Proverbs in Scots* as 'Better to wow over middin, nor over mure'.

Better twa skaiths than ae sorrow.
Losses can be repaired but a sorrow can break one's spirit.

Better wear shoon than wear sheets.
It is better to be wearing shoes in the first place than end up
ill in bed, i.e. prevention is the best kind of medicine.

Better you laugh than I greet.
I would rather be ridiculed for not doing a thing than do it
and be sorry for it.

**Between three and thirteen thraw the woodie when its
green.**
Train the minds of children when they are young.

Bide weel, betide weel.
If you wait patiently you will fare well.

Biggin and bairns marrying are arrant wasters.
Building houses and children marrying are expensive
undertakings.

**Birk will burn be it burn drawn, sauch will sab if it
were simmer sawn.**
Birch will burn even if it is soaking, but willow will hiss even
if it has been sawn in the summer and allowed to dry for the
winter. Basically this means that everything will revert to its
natural type.

Bitin' and scartin' are Scotch folk's wooin'.

Blue are the hills that are far away.
Distance improves how things appear. In John Buchan's
Watcher by the Threshold (1902), he mentions that this 'is an
owercome in the countryside'.

Bode for a silk gown and ye'll get a sleeve o't.
Set your sights high if you hope to achieve anything.

Bourdna wi' bawty lest he bite ye.
A warning not to fool with your superiors.

Bread's house skail'd never.
A full or hospitable house never wants visitors.

Butter to butter's nae kitchen.
Like to like provides no relish. Often used by cheeky males
when they see women kissing each other.

Ca' a cow to the ha' and she'll rin to the byre.
People feel more comfortable in familiar surroundings.

Ca' again you're no a ghaist.
A welcoming invitation for a person to call again, i.e. their visits are not unwelcome like those of a ghost.

Ca' canny and ye'll break nae graith.
Take care and you won't come a cropper. Literally, drive slowly and you won't overstrain your harness.

Ca' canny, lad, ye're but a new-come cooper.
A warning to those who are new at a profession to take things cautiously, hinting that more experience or information might be needed than is immediately apparent.

Cadgers are aye cracking o' crook-saddles.
'Crook-saddles' are those used for supporting panniers. Professionals are very apt to talk too much of their profession.

Caff and draff is gude enough for aivers.
Caff and draff are brewer's grains, and are plenty good enough for horses. A suggestion that common food suits unsophisticated people.

Can do is easily carried about wi' ane.
Knowledge accompanies you wherever you are.

Canna has nae craft.
To the person who is unwilling, instruction is useless.

Carrick for a man, Kyle for a coo, Cunningham for corn and ale, and Galloway for woo'.
A local saying from the South West of Scotland.

Carrying saut to Dysart and puddings to Tranent.
A Scottish version of the English saying 'Carrying coals to Newcastle', i.e. carrying out a redundant task.

Cast a cat ower the house and she'll fa' on her feet.
Said of people on whom good luck always seems to shine.

Cast not a clout till May be out.
A warning not to get rid of one's winter clothing until the end of May.

Cast the cat ower him.
It was believed at one time that a cure for a raging fever was to cast a cat over the patient. The saying is applied to those heard telling such outrageous stories as if they were raving through fever.

Cats and carlins sit i' the sun, but fair maidens sit within.
A suggestion that over exposure to the sun is not good for young girls. In olden days, girls were supposed to look more attractive if they were pale.

Cauld kail het again is aye pat tasted.
Something generally does not improve by repetition. Often said when someone starts to tell the same story again.

Chalk's no shears.
There is a great difference between merely marking out on the cloth a desired pattern from actually cutting it, i.e. planning to do something is not the same as actually doing it.

Changes o' wark is a lightening o' hearts.
A change in routine relieves the monotony and so revives
flagging spirits. A change is as good as a rest.

Cheatery game will aye kythe.
Wrongdoing will always come to light. Be sure your sins will
find you out.

Choose your wife on Saturday, not on Sunday.
A suggestion that a man should choose a wife for her good
qualities and usefulness which are in evidence in her daily
labours, rather than for her appearance and manners in her
Sunday best outfit.

Choose yer wife wi' her nightcap on.
A proverb giving a warning similar to that above.

Christiecleek will come to ye.
This has been used as a phrase of terror for centuries in
Scotland, particularly by parents trying to frighten unruly
children into behaving themselves. In fourteenth-century
Scotland, a combination of wars, famine and anarchy forced
some Highlanders to turn to cannibalism. One such
character was Christie, a gang leader, who according to
stories attacked his victims using a large iron hook, or 'cleek',
to drag them down. Hence he earned the terryifing nickname 'Christiecleek'. He is said to have evaded capture and
to have eventually prospered as a merchant when times
improved.

**Come a' to Jock Fool's house and ye'll get bread and
cheese.**
This saying is spoken sarcastically to those who invite people
indiscriminately.

Come unca'd, sits unserved.
The uninvited guest is an unwelcome one. A warning to all
gatecrashers.

Common saw sindle lies.
Common sayings seldom lie. This would seem to be at
variance with another proverb 'Rumour is a common liar'.

Corbies dinna pike out corbie's een.
Wrongdoers tend not to wrong each other.

Crab without a cause, mease without mends.
A person who is angry without cause will try to appease
without making amends.

Craft maun hae claes, but truth gaes naked.
The former needs to be disguised whereas the latter is self
evident.

Curses mak the tod fat.
Curses and threats in themselves do not make anything
happen; action is needed if things are to be resolved.

Daffin' does naething.
Playing accomplishes nothing.

Daily wearing needs yearly beiting.
Constant use brings with it constant renewing, i.e. you cannot expect to wear the same clothes daily without having to renew them once a year.

Dame, deem warily, ye watna wytes yoursel.
Don't be hasty to judge others, when you are not sure who may find fault with yourself.

Dammin' and lavin' is gude sure fishing.
The technique of "Dammin' and lavin" is used by poachers as a way of catching fish in small rivulets, first by damming and thereby diverting the course of the stream, and then by laving or throwing out the water so as to get them.

Danger past, God forgotten.
Many people pray when facing adversity but soon forget their religion when the danger has passed.

Daughters and dead fish are kittle keeping wares.
This saying suggests that daughters should be married and dead fish eaten otherwise they will both spoil.

Dawted daughters mak dawly wives.
Daughters who have been doted upon tend to make untidy wives as they are unused to doing any work around the house.

Death and drink-draining are near neighbours.
Not so much a warning of the dangers of drinking to excess, as an allusion to the wakes or amount of drinking that used to be common after funerals.

Death at ae door and heirship at the other.

Death comes in and speirs nae questions.
Death visits us unannounced and treats everyone alike.

Deil be in the house that ye're beguiled in.
Said as a compliment meaning that the person thus addressed is considered to be so shrewd that only the Devil in person could deceive them.

Deil be in the pock that ye cam in.
A wish that evil should befall the listener.

Deil mend ye if your leg were broken.
A saying of similar sentiment to the above one.

Deil speed them that speir, and ken fu' weel.
To the devil with those people who ask questions to which they already have the answers.

Did ye ever fit counts wi' him?
Do not count upon someone's friendship until you have had financial transactions with them.

Ding down the nest and the rooks will flee away.
Destroy a villain's hideout and he'll soon disappear. Unfortunately this proverb was used during the Reformation with regard to the destruction of the collegiate churches, abbeys and cathedrals.

Dinna bow to bawtie, lest he bite.
Familiarity breeds contempt.

Dinna cast awa' the cog when the cow flings.
Do not give up at the first misfortune – try, try again.

Dinna dry the burn because it wat your feet.
Do not remove a useful thing because of some minor
inconvenience.

Dinna gut your fish till ye get them.
Advice not to live on expectations, as one can never be
certain what will happen in the future. Another version of
'Don't count your chickens until they've hatched.'

Dinna meddle wi' the deil and the laird's bairns.
In both cases it was known that anyone doing so was sure to
come off worst.

Dinna open yer mooth tae fill ither fowks.
A warning against gossiping.

Dinna scald your mouth wi' ither folk's kail.
Don't poke your nose into other people's business – it will
only end up hurting you.

**Dinna sigh for him, but send for him: if he be
unhanged he'll come.**
A cry against procrastination. Do not just wish for something
or speak about it – do it.

**Dinna speak o' a raip to a chiel whase faither was
hang'd.**
Think before you speak, or you may inadvertently put your
foot in it.

Dinna touch him on the sair heal.
A plea for tact and diplomacy. Do not speak to him about a
certain subject on which he is known to be sensitive.

Dit your mouth wi' your meat.
Close your mouth with your food. A suggestion that someone stop gossiping.

Do as the coo o' Forfar did, tak a stannin' drink.
A cow in Forfar stopped while passing a doorway and drank a tub of ale which had been placed on the doorstep to cool. The owner of the ale tried to sue the owner of the cow for the value of the ale consumed by the beast. However, a local baillie gave the decision in favour of the cow's owner, because he decreed that since the ale had been drunk by the cow while it was standing by the door, it must be considered as a deoch-an-dorius (Stirrup cup) for which no charge could be made, according to the rules of ancient Scottish hospitality.

Dool and an ill life soon mak an auld wife.
Sorrow and an evil life soon age a woman.

Do on the hill as ye wad do in the ha'.
Be consistent in your actions. Do in public as you would in private.

Double charges rive cannons.
Moderation in all things is the best policy, as excesses can be dangerous.

Do weel, an' doubt nae man; do ill an' doubt a' men.
The person with a guilty conscience can trust no one.

Do your turn weel, and nane will speir what time ye took.
A suggestion that well-done work is appreciated rather than the speed at which it is done.

Draff he sought, but drink was his errand.
While asking for one thing, a person may really be after something else.

Dree out the inch, when ye have thol'd the span.
When you have suffered patiently for a long while, don't give up just as the end is in sight.

Drink and drouth come na aye thegither.
Things do not always occur when you want them to.

Dry bargains bode ill.
In the past, a deal was considered unlucky unless it was ratified with a drink.

Eagles catch nae fleas.
A saying applied to conceited people who affect disdain for
small details.

**East and wast the sign o' a blast; north and south the
sign o' a drouth.**
Weather forecasting according to the direction of the
prevailing wind.

East or west, hame is best.
Often said after returning from a journey or holiday.

Easy learning the cat the road to the kirn.
It is easier to learn something when your natural inclinations
lie along similar lines.

Eaten meat is ill to pay.
We do not like having to pay for things already consumed
and forgotten.

Eat in measure and defy the doctor.
For a healthy life – moderation in all things.

Eats meat, an's never fed; wears claes, an's never cled.
No matter how well some people are provided for, they
never appear to look any the better for it.

Eat-weel's Drink-weel's brither.
Good eating and drinking should go side by side.

E'ening grey and a morning red, put on your hat or ye'll weet your head; E'ening red an' a morning grey is a taiken o' a bonny day.
Red sky in morning, shepherd's warning;
Red sky at night, shepherd's delight.

E'ening orts are gude morning's fodder.
'Orts' are rejected foodstuffs, i.e. a thing which is rejected now, may be acceptable or even desirable at a later date.

Eident youth maks easy age.
A person will reap the rewards of a hard-working youth in later years.

Eild and poortith are a fair burden for ae back.
Old age and poverty are a sore burden for one person to bear.

Eith keeping the castle that's no beseiged.
It is easy to be in charge when there are no problems to face.

Eith learned, soon forgotten.
What is soon learned is forgotten just as quickly.

Eith working when will's at hame.
It is easier to get work done when the heart is willing.

Enough's enough o' bread and cheese.
Too much of a good thing is not good.

Even a haggis will run downhill.
Spoken when a cowardly action is observed. It does not take a particularly brave soldier to charge downhill.

Even stands his cap the day, for a' that.
This saying is used when we consider that all that we can say against a great person cannot possibly do them any harm. It was reputedly used by a minister in concluding a sermon in which he had most fervently preached against the supremacy of the Pope.

Every ane loups the dyke where it's laighest.
Everyone does what comes easiest to them.

Every craw thinks his ain bird whitest.
Every parent thinks well of their own children.

Every land has its laigh; every corn has its ain cauff.
This proverb has been given two meanings. In Kelly's *Scottish Proverbs* (1721), it is recorded as meaning that 'every country hath its own laws, customs, and usages'. However Hislop's *Proverbs of Scotland* (1862) gives a different interpretation, namely 'everything may be found fault with; and silly objections be raised against the most valuable and useful things'.

Every man bows to the bush he gets beild frae.
Everyone has to pay their respects to those who protect them.

Every man buckles his belt his ain gate.
Everyone works in their own way.

Every man can guide an ill wife weel but him that has her.
It is always easy for those not in a particular situation to comment upon it.

Every man can tout best on his ain horn.
Everyone knows best how to tell their own story.

Every man for his ain hand, as Henry Wynd fought.
Around 1392 two clans fought a battle with thirty a side, in
the presence of the King, on the North Inch of Perth. One
man went missing and his place was filled by a wee bandy-
legged citizen called Henry Wynd (or Gow Chrom as the
Highlanders called him). He fought well and greatly
contributed to the outcome of the battle without knowing on
whose side he had fought.

Every man has his ain bubbly-jock.
We all have our own problems and crosses to bear.
According to popular folk legend, a man described as a
simpleton working for a farmer was asked by a visitor if he
was happy. He said that he was comfortable, well fed and
well provided for, but upset because the turkey-cock didn't
like him and would chase him on sight.

**Every man has his ain draff poke, though some hang
eider than others.**
Every person has their own faults, though for some these are
more apparent than in others.

**Every man's man had a man, and that gar'd the
Treve fa'.**
The Treve, or Threve, was a very strong castle which
belonged to the Black Douglases. The governor of the castle
left a deputy in charge, and he in turn a substitute, by whose
negligence the castle was taken and burned.

Every sow to her ain trough.
Everyone to their own place, i.e. you should not depend
upon others.

Everything has an end, and a pudding has twa.

Everything has its time, and sae has a rippling-kame.
A 'rippling-kame' is a coarse comb used in the flax industry.
The proverb means that there is a time proper for
everything.

Every wight has his weird, and we maun a' dee when our day comes.
No person can avoid what is destined to happen to them.

Facts are chiels that winna ding.
Facts cannot be denied.

Faint heart ne'er wan fair lady.

Fair exchange is nae robbery.

Fair fa' gude drink, for it gars folk speak as they think.
Good luck to good drink, for it causes people to speak their minds.

Fair fa' the wife, and weel may she spin, that counts aye the lawin' wi' a pint to come in.
Good luck to the hostess who includes a pint still to come when it is time to reckon up.

Fair fa' you, and that's nae fleaching.
Good wishes meant sincerely.

Fair folk are aye foisonless.

Fair hair may hae foul roots.
A warning that outward appearances can be deceptive.

Fair maidens wear nae purses.
Despite their legendary meanness, this was a phrase commonly used by Scotsmen at one time, when a woman offered to pay in mixed company.

Fann'd fires and forced love ne'er did weel.
A warning not to force things that do not come naturally.

Far ahint that mayna follow, an' far before that canna look back.
A warning not to let oneself stray too far from the mainstream.

Far-awa fowls hae fair feathers.
Sometimes the further away something is or the harder it is to get makes something appear more desirable than it actually is.

Far sought and dear bought is gude for ladies.
The harder it has been to obtain something the more favourably it will be looked upon.

Farthest frae the kirk aye soonest at it.
This saying is in contradiction to those who are 'near the kirk but far frae grace'.

Fashious fools are easiest flisket.
Troublesome people are most easily offended.

Fat paunches bode lean pows.
Overfull stomachs lead to empty skulls.

Fausehood maks ne'er a fair hinder-end.
Falsehood is bound to be exposed in the long run.

Feckless folk are aye fain o' ane anither.
Silly people are always fond of each other.

Feckless fools should keep canny tongues.
Silly people should watch what they say, lest it land them in trouble.

Feed a cauld, but hunger a colic.
Homespun medical advice.

Fiddlers, dogs, and flesh-flies come aye to feasts unca'd.
Those who live off others will always turn up uninvited.

Fiddlers' wives and gamesters' drink are free to ilka body.
The suggestion is that the fiddler and gamester are both too preoccupied to look after their own things properly.

Fill fu' and haud fu', maks a stark man.
Plenty of food and drink makes a strong man.

Fire is gude for the fireside.
All things are good when they are in their proper places or put to their proper uses.

Fish maun soom thrice.
First in water, second in sauce, and third in wine.

Fleas and a girning wife are waukrife bedfellows.
A man will get little sleep if he shares his bed with fleas or a fretful wife.

Fleying a bird is no the gate to grip it.
Literally – frightening a bird is not the way to catch it. This saying is often applied to bringing up children, implying that constant threatening will not improve their behaviour.

Fools and bairns should ne'er see half done wark.
They may mistakenly judge the finished product by the state of the incomplete project.

Fools mak feasts and wise men eat them.
This was reputedly said to the Duke of Lauderdale by a rude guest. Being a great wit he immediately retorted 'Aye and wise men mak proverbs, and fools repeat them!' So beware!

For as gude again, like Sunday milk.
A respectable countrywoman would not sell her milk on a
Sunday, but would give it for as good again. This saying is
applied to those whose kindness we suspect to be mercenary
in its origins.

For a tint thing, care na.
Do not waste your time worrying about lost opportunities.

**For better acquaintance sake, as Sir John Ramsay said
when he drank to his father.**
On returning home after many years abroad, Sir John
Ramsay accidentally met his father, who did not know him.
He invited him to take a glass of wine with him and drank to
better acquaintance.

Fortune aye favours the active and bauld.
You only get out of life what you are willing to put in.

For want o' a steek a shoe may be tint.
A stitch in time saves nine.

**Four churches together and only one steeple, Is an
emblem quite apt of the thrift of the people.**
A witty description of Dundee by Thomas Hood.

Frae the teeth forward.
Said of someone who speaks without great conviction, i.e. he
speaks from the lips and not from the heart.

**Fresh fish and unwelcome guests stink before they're
three days auld.**

Friday flit short time sit.
It is considered unlucky to move house on a Friday.

**Friends are like fiddle-strings, they maunna be
screwed ower ticht.**

Gae to bed wi' the lamb and rise wi' the laverock.
Early to bed, early to rise!

Gae to the deil and he'll bishop you.
Said to somebody who is considered to be so bad that the
devil would grant them high office.

Gathering gear is weel liket wark.
Acquiring wealth is pleasant employment.

**Gaunting bodes wanting ane o' things three – sleep,
meat, or gude companie.**
Yawning was traditionally said to be caused by a lack of one
of the above three things.

Gaunting gaes frae man to man.
The act of yawning is infectious.

Gawsie cow, gudely calf.
Handsome mother, goodly daughter.

Gaylie would be better.
Said when a person is not feeling well, i.e. gaylie or 'pretty
well' would be better than they presently feel.

**Geese tae the sea, guid weather tae be; Geese tae the
hull, guid weather tae spill.**
A popular weather rhyme from Angus.

Gentlemen are unco scant when a wabster gets a leddy.
Another proverbial slight against the weaving fraternity, suggesting that there must be few men around when one actually attracts a woman.

Get the word o' soon rising an' ye may lie in bed a' day.
Obtain a good reputation and you can get away with misbehaving without people suspecting you.

Get what you can, and keep what you hae, that's the way to get rich.

Gibbie's grace – deil claw the clungiest.
Devil take the hungriest.

Gie a bairn his will, and a whelp its fill, and nane o' them will e'er do weel.
Giving in to the demands of children will only spoil them.

Gie a beggar a bed, and he'll pay you wi' a louse.
It is pointless trying to help some people.

Gie him a hole and he'll find a pin.
Give the person a chance or opportunity and he will take advantage of it.

Gie is a gude fellow, but he soon wearies.
One becomes tired of always giving.

Gie ye meat, drink, and claes, and ye'll beg among your friends.
Said unkindly to people who get everything and are still not satisfied.

Giff gaff maks gude friends.
Give and take between people helps to build a good relationship.

Glib i' the tongue is aye glaiket at the heart.
Don't trust those who are silver tongued, as it betrays a
deceitful heart.

Glum folk's no easily guided.
It is difficult to manage morose people.

**God be wi' the gude laird o' Balmaghie, for he ne'er
took mair frae a poor man than a' that he had.**
The good laird was obviously not noted for his generosity.

God help you to a hutch, for ye'll never get a mailing.
Said to someone considered to be incompetent: that they
may be able to scratch a small living, but their lack of
abilities will never secure them a fortune.

**God keep ill gear out o' my hands; for if my hands
ance get it, my heart winna part wi't, – sae prayed the
gude Earl of Eglinton.**
A prayer not to be led into temptation.

**God keep the cat out o' our gate, for the hens canna
flee.**
A plea to be spared danger, because the speaker cannot
defend themselves.

God ne'er sent the mouth, but he sent the meat wi't.
A plea to trust in God to provide what is necessary in life.

God's aye kind to fu' folks and bairns.
A comment on how the flexibility of a drunk's limbs helps
them to avoid injury.

God shapes the back for the burden.

Great barkers are nae biters.
Don't be frightened of those who make a lot of noise about things – their bark is worse than their bite, i.e. their actions are not as drastic as their words.

Great pains and little gains soon mak a man weary.

Greed is envy's auldest brither: scraggy wark they mak thegither.

Gude ale needs nae wisp.
In days gone by, a wisp of straw was stuck on the roof of a country house to show that ale was sold there. But if the ale was good, no such advertising was necessary as word of mouth would guarantee a full house.

Gude cheer and cheap gars mony haunt the house.
A hospitable house will never want for visitors.

Gude folks are scarce, you'll take care of one.
This saying is spoken to those who carefully protect themselves against bad weather, or who cowardly shun any dangers or problems.

Gude gear gangs into little bouk.
Good things come in small packages.

Gut nae fish till ye get them.
Another version of 'Don't count your chickens until they've hatched'.

Ha' binks are sliddery.
Literally this means that the benches in the entrance hall of a grand house are slippery, i.e. the favour of one's superiors is always uncertain.

Had you sic a shoe on ilka foot, it would gar you shackle.
If you had my troubles to bear you too would look miserable.

Hae, gars a deaf man hear.
Some people are only deaf when it is convenient.

Hae you gear, or hae you nane, tine heart and a' is gone.
Without heart, everything is pointless.

Hain'd gear helps weel.
Savings are of great assistance.

Half acres bear aye gude corn.
Those who have least often make the most of it.

'Hame's hamely', quo' the deil when he fand himsel in the Court o' Session.
The Court of Session is the supreme civil tribunal in Scotland which was established in 1532. In his introduction to Henderson's *Scottish Proverbs* the poet William Motherwell said of this saying 'Nothing more bitter was ever uttered ... against our Supreme Court of Judicature.' No comment!

Hand-in-use is father o' lear.
Practical experience is the best way of learning something.

Hand ower head, as men took the covenant.
This saying alludes to the manner in which the covenant was violently taken by over 60,000 people in Edinburgh in 1638.

Hang a thief when he's young, and he'll no steal when he's auld.
This was reputedly a favourite saying of Robert MacQueen (1722–99), Lord Chief Justice Braxfield, who invariably acted upon its teaching.

Hap an' a ha'penny is world's gear enough.
Happiness and modest means are all that one needs in this life.

Happy man be his dool.
A good wish – that happiness be the greatest affliction sent him.

Happy's the maid that's married to a mitherless son.
An old-fashioned jibe at mothers-in-law.

Haste maks waste, and waste maks want, and want maks strife between the gudeman and the gudewife.

Haud the hank in your ain hand.
Do the difficult part yourself.

Hawks winna pike oot hawks' een.
Wrongdoers generally do not wrong each other.

He bides as fast as a cat does to a saucer.
A saying applied to mercenary characters – that they will stay as long as there is something for them.

He blaws in his lug fu' brawly.
To 'blaw the lug' is to praise a person in an extravagant manner.

He can say 'My Jo', and think it no.
He can be complimentary in his speech but not in his intentions.

He ca's me scabbed because I winna ca' him sca'd.
A person has tried to make his opponent lose his temper but, in failing to do so, has ended up losing his own.

He comes oftener wi' the rake than the shool.
Again, said of a mercenary type, who comes to take more often than to give.

He counts his ha'penny gude siller.
A man may give a small gratuity but have an exaggerated idea of his own generosity.

He cuts awfu' near the wood.
To 'cut near the wood' is to drive a hard bargain.

He doesna aye ride when he saddles his horse.
He does not always carry through everything that he starts.

He doesna ken a B frae a bull's foot.
He is exceptionally ignorant on the matter.

He eats the calf i' the cow's wame.
Said of someone who lives off their expectations.

He gangs lang barefoot that waits for dead men's shoon.
Spoken as a warning to those who expect to inherit on the death of another.

He got his mother's malison the day he was married.
Said of a man who has a bad wife.

He has a bee in his bonnet-lug.
Said of somebody who has a particular preoccupation of their own.

He has a hearty hand for gieing a hungry meltith.
He is very charitable.

He has a hole beneath his nose that winna let his back be rough.
He is so fond of his food that he does not have the money left to make his back 'rough', or well clothed.

He has a saw for a' sairs.

He has been rowed in his mither's sark tail.
The Scots equivalent of saying that a man is tied to his mother's apron strings.

He has coup'd the muckle pat into the little.
Said sarcastically of those who claim to have achieved the impossible.

He has gi'en up a trade and ta'en to stravaigin'.
To stravaig is to walk about idly. This saying is said in fun of those who have retired from business to live comfortably.

He has gotten his kail through the reek.
To meet with severe reprehension.

He has got the heavy end of him.
In an argument he has the better of his opponent.

He has help'd me out o' a deadlift.
He has helped me in an emergency.

He has licket the butter aff my bread.
He has taken away my business.

He has made a moonlight flitting.
He has removed house in the middle of the night to avoid paying any rent owed.

He has need o' a clean pow that ca's his neighbour nitty-now.
Do not criticise others unless you are perfect yourself.

He has ower mony greedy gleds o' his ain.
A man has too many family claims upon his resources to enable him to help any strangers.

He jumped at it, like a cock at a grosset.
He seized the opportunity without a moment's hesitation.

He kens his ain groats amang other folk's kail.
Said of someone who is acutely aware of his own interests.

He left his siller in his ither pocket.
Said of people who try to get out of paying their fair share.

He'll gang mad on a horse wha's proud on a pownie.
Spoken of those who let the least bit of power go to their heads.

He'll hae enough some day, when his mouth's fu' o' mools.
Spoken of greedy people who will never be satisfied as long as they are alive.

He'll kythe in his ain colours yet.
He will appear as himself, and not in disguise.

He'll neither dance nor haud the candle.
He will neither join in nor let others do so.

He'll no gie an inch o' his will for a span o' his thrift.
His wishes must be satisfied, no matter the expense.

He'll no gie the head for the washing.
To 'keep the head for the washing' is to retain possession of
an article which has either been made to measure, or handed
in for repair, until payment is received.

He'll tell it to nae mair than he meets.
He will tell it to everyone he meets.

He lo'ed mutton weel that lick'd where the ewie lay.
A humorous remark made to those who scrape the bottom
of their dish or drink the very last drops from a glass.

Help is gude at a'thing, except at the cog.
Help is always appreciated, except when taking one's food.

**He may be trusted wi' a house fu' o' unbored
millstanes.**
He cannot be trusted at all.

**He needs a lang-shanket spoon that sups kail wi' the
deil, or a Fifer.**
Few people were thought to be as cunning and wily as those
from the Kingdom of Fife, and this proverb serves as a
warning to be on one's guard with such people.

He never lies but when the holly's green.
Holly being an evergreen, this saying is applied to a person
who never tells the truth.

He reives the kirk to theek the quire.
Literally, he steals from the church to roof the choir, or robs
Peter to pay Paul.

He rides on the riggin' o't.
He goes to a great extreme.

He rides sicker that never fa's.
The person who never makes a mistake is sure of themself.

**He's a fool that asks ower muckle, but he's a greater
fool that gies it.**

**He's a fool that marries at Yule; for when the bairn's
to bear the corn's to shear.**
Old-fashioned rural family planning advice.

He's as bold as a Lammermuir lion.
He's not very bold at all. The Lammermuir hills is a pastoral
area not noted for wild animals, but a 'lion' is a local
nickname for a sheep.

He's as fu's a fiddler.
He's drunk.

He's awfu' big ahint the door.
He is very brave when there is no occasion for it.

He's either a' honey or a' dirt.
He is either exceedingly kind and affectionate or quite the
reverse.

He's failed wi' a fu' hand.
Said when a person declares themself bankrupt and hence
does not have to pay off creditors immediately.

He's got his nose in a gude kail pat.
Often said of someone who has married a person of wealth.

He's horn deaf on that side o' his head.
Meaning that he has made up his mind upon the matter in question.

He sleeps as dogs do when wives sift meal.
The person is very sharp and figuratively sleeps with one eye open.

He's like a bagpipe, ne'er heard till his wame's fu.

He's like a cow in an unco loan.
He is out of place.

He's like the smith's dog – so weel used to the sparks that he'll no burn.
Said of people who are so used to drinking alcohol, that they never seem to be the worse for it.

He's mair buirdly i' the back than i' the brain.
Suggesting the person's strength is of a physical rather than a mental nature.

He snites his nose in his neighbour's dish to get the brose himsel.
An all too vividly expressive proverb, used when someone will harm others to benefit personally.

He starts at straes, and lets windlins gae.
Said of nit-picking people who are so intent on correcting trifling mistakes, that they miss the important things.

He stumbles at a strae and loups ower a linn.
Another variation on the preceding proverb.

He's weel stocket there ben that will neither borrow nor lend.
A person must be comfortably provided for if they can afford to dispense with any help.

He that blaws in the stour fills his am een.
The individual who creates trouble is likely to end up in it himself.

He that can hear Dumbuck may hear Dumbarton.
A saying local to Glasgow. Dumbuck hill in Argyll is farther from Glasgow than Dumbarton. Hence, the saying is applied to those who are better acquainted with circumstances than they pretend to be, but who, in their search for more information, give themselves away.

He that cheats me ance, shame fa' him; he that cheats me twice, shame fa' me.
A reminder to learn by one's mistakes.

He that counts a' costs will ne'er put plough i' the grand.
A plea for positive thinking. The person who weighs up all the possible difficulties will never get around to doing anything.

He that follows freits, freits will follow him.
The person who looks for portents of the future will find themself dogged by them. This proverb must date from around the sixteenth century, as it first appears in J. Pinkerton's *Scottish Tragic Ballads* (1781) as 'Wha luik to freits. My master deir, Freits will ay follow them.'

He that gets gear before he gets wit is but a short time maister o't.
A warning to any winner of the National Lottery. A fool and his money are soon parted.

He that has ae sheep in a flock will like a' the lave the better for't.
When our kith and kin enter a group or club, we wish all the other members well because of their relationship.

He that has a muckle nose thinks ilka ane speaks o't.
People who have a secret to hide are always suspicious of others.

He that has a wife has a master.

He that has lost a wife and sixpence has lost sixpence.

He that has routh o' butter may butter his bread on baith sides.
The person who is well supplied with a commodity can afford to be generous with it.

He that hews abune his head may get a spail in his e'e.
He who aims at things beyond his power or abilities may be injured in the process.

He that invented the maiden first hanselled her.
The 'maiden' was an early form of guillotine and was supposedly so-called because many men had lain with her but none had got the better of her. There is some doubt to the truth of the foundations of the above proverb, but it was reputed that James, Earl of Morton, who invented the maiden was also the first person to suffer by it. A proverb which perhaps owes more to poetic justice than historical truth.

He that lends money to a friend has a double loss.
In doing so he loses both his money and hence his friend.

He that lippens to lent ploughs his land will lang lie lea.
The person who relies upon the favours of others is open to being greatly disappointed.

He that marries a widow and twa dochters has three back doors to his house.
Another warning against marrying a widow, this time suggesting that if she already has children the new husband will also end up providing for them as well.

He that meddles wi' tulzies may come in for the redding stroke.
Anyone willing to meddle with quarrelsome people is likely to come off worst.

He that plays wi' fools and bairns maun e'en play at the chucks.
When a man mixes with individuals less intelligent than himself he must adapt his behaviour accordingly.

He that rides ahint anither doesna saddle when he pleases.
Those who depend upon others are not always at liberty to do things when they would choose.

He that's aught the cow gangs nearest the tail.
The owner of something should be willing to risk more for it than anyone else.

He that's far frae his gear is near his skaith.
A warning to people to keep a weather eye on their own property.

He that's ill o' his harboury is gude at the way-kenning.
An unwilling host is likely to be able to tell the unwanted guest the times of the next trains home!

He that sits upon a stane is twice fain.
He is glad to sit down through tiredness but glad again to rise because the stone is hard and uncomfortable.

He that sleeps wi' dogs maun rise wi' fleas.
Those who keep bad company cannot expect to remain
unaffected, i.e. guilt by association.

He that spares to speak spares to speed.
The person who is reticent to speak about their own talents
when an opportunity arises for advancement does themself
harm.

**He that's scant o' wind shouldna meddle wi' the
chanter.**
A saying applied to those who take on a task which is greater
than they can cope with.

**He that stumbles twice at ae stane deserves to break
his shin bane.**
The person who does not learn by their mistakes deserves
everything that happens to them.

He that tines his siller is thought to hae tint his wit.
Meaning that a person who willingly loses or risks losing
money must have lost all sense.

He that will to Cupar maun to Cupar.
A reflection upon obstinate people. Another line is
sometimes added: 'Aye better gang than be ta'en', or 'Sae
gang tae Cupar an' be damned!'

**He that winna lout and lift preen will ne'er be worth a
great.**
The person who refuses to bother with the small things will
never be wealthy. Look after the pennies and the pounds will
look after themselves.

He that winna when he may, shanna when he wad.
Spoken of somebody who doesn't want a thing until he can
no longer have it.

He that would eat the fruit maun climb the tree.
There is no gain without pain.

Het kail cauld, nine days auld, spell ye that in four letters.
A well known children's riddle, the key to which is the four letter word 'that'.

He watsna whilk end o' him's upmost.
Said of someone who is unsure if they are on their head or their heels. They are in a turmoil.

He wha marries a maiden marries a pockfu' o' pleasure; he wha marries a widow marries a pockfu' o' pleasure.
Yet more proverbial marriage guidance, warning of the dangers of marrying a widow.

He would skin a louse for the tallow o't.
Applied to anyone who is extremely miserly.

He would tine his lugs if they were not tacked to him.
Spoken of the forgetful.

High trees show mair leaves than fruit.
A disparaging remark sometimes made to tall people.

His auld brass will buy her a new pan.
Said of young women who marry older men, suggesting that when their husbands die, they will use his money to attract a younger one.

His head will ne'er fill his faither's bannet.
An expression of doubt that the son will live up to the reputation of his father.

His wame thinks his wizen's cut.
Said when someone is exceedingly hungry.

Hunger's gude kitchen to a cauld potato, but a wet divot to the lowe o' love.
Hunger makes any food acceptable, but it is a damper on one's love life.

I ance gied a dog his hansel, an' he was hang'd ere night.
An excuse for not giving someone a gratuity, lest it lead to harm in some way.

I bake nae bread by your shins.
I am under no obligation to you.

I canna afford ye baith tale and lugs.
Said as a rebuke to an inattentive person who has asked for a story to be repeated.

I canna sell the cow an' sup the milk.
The equivalent of not being able to have one's cake and eat it.

I carena whether the fire gae about the roast, or the roast gae about the fire, if the meat be ready.
Spoken by someone who does not care how a thing is done, so long as the desired end is reached.

I deny that wi' baith hands and a' my teeth.
I emphatically deny that.

If a lee could hae chokit you, ye wad hae been dead langsyne.
A humorous way of suggesting that you suspect someone of telling a falsehood.

If a man's gaun down the brae ilka ane gies him a jundie.
Beware! People can be very cruel to those who have fallen upon hard times.

If a' thing's true that's nae lee.
A saying denoting disbelief in some unlikely story.

If a' things were to be done twice ilka ane wad be wise.
Practice makes perfect, as we learn by our mistakes.

If a' your hums and haws were hams and haggises, the parish needna fear a dearth.
A warning against indecision and procrastination.

If he gies a duck he expects a goose.
Spoken of people who expect more in return than they are willing to give.

If I canna kep geese, I can kep gaislins.
If I cannot reap revenge upon a person, I will do so upon his offspring.

If I come I maun bring my stool wi' me.
As I have not been invited, I had better bring my own seat.

If 'ifs' an' 'buts' were kettles an' pans, there would be nae use for tinklers.
If it were not for the 'ifs' and 'buts' in this world, we would all soon be rich.

If I had a dog as daft as you I would shoot him.
Said as a warning to people to stop fooling around.

If it be a faut it's nae ferlie.
It is no wonder, as no other result should have been expected.

If it sair me to wear it, it may sair you to look at.
A rebuke to people who criticise others' dress.

If it winna sell it winna sour.
Said of good things; that they are worth keeping.

If marriages are made in heaven you twa hae few friends there.
Spoken of couples who are always fighting.

If the auld wife hadna been in the oven hersel, she ne'er wad hae thought o' looking for her dochter there.
Unless a person has already been guilty of some crime themselves, it is unlikely that they would suspect another of it.

If the lift fa' the laverocks will be smoored.
Said as a rejoinder when someone mentions some highly improbable turn of events.

If this be a feast I hae been at mony.
Said by a person to imply that they are not impressed by the treatment they are receiving.

If wishes were horses beggars wad ride, and a' the warld be drowned in pride.
This proverb is thought to date from before 1628 and is recorded in Carmichaell's *Proverbs in Scots* as 'And wishes were horses pure men wald ryde.'

If you dinna haud him he'll do't a'.
Said sarcastically of a lazy person.

If you dinna see the bottom, dinna wade.
Do not undertake anything until you can clearly see what you're getting yourself into.

If ye had as little money as ye hae manners ye would be the poorest man o' a' your kin.
Said as a reprimand to someone who behaves in a rude manner.

If ye sell your purse to your wife, gie her your breeks to the bargain.
A saying used in the days when men were principle wage earners of the family, and were seen as being 'head of the household.' It suggests that if a man gives up financial control to his wife she will become head of the family.

If you would be a merchant fine, beware o' auld horses, herring, and wine.
Proverbially speaking the first will die, the second will stink, and the third sour.

I hae a good bow, but it's i' the castle.
Said of those who are always claiming that they could perform heroic deeds, if only they had remembered to bring some necessary article with them which they know is not near at hand.

I hae a heid an' so has a stair.

I hae a Scotch tongue in my head – if they speak I'se answer.

I hae gi'en a stick to break my ain head.
I have undertaken something which is to my own disadvantage.

I hae seen as fu' a haggis toom'd on the midden.
A disparaging remark about an article. I have seen as good an article thrown away.

I hae seen mair than I hae eaten, else ye wadna be here.
Spoken as a sharp rebuke to someone who doubts a statement of which the speaker has been an eye witness.

I ken by my cog how my cow's milk'd.
I can judge how a thing has been done by its very appearance.

I ken by your half-tale what your hale tale means.
I am quite capable of reading between the lines to get the full story.

Ilka blade o' grass keeps its ain drap o' dew.
Everyone has their own business to attend to.

Ilka doorstep has its ain slippery stane.
Every thing has its own problems.

I'll big nae sandy mills wi' you.
Literally, I will not build any sandcastles with you. I will not join you in any project.

Ill comes upon waur's back.
One bad fortune tends to follow another.

I'll do as the man did when he sell't his land.
This means that the person will not do it again, for selling one's land or assets is something one rarely does twice.

Ill flesh ne'er made good broo.
Literally, bad meat never made good soup. A bad person cannot be expected to perform a good act.

I'll gie ye a sark fu' o' sair bones.
I'll give you a beating.

I'll gie ye let-a-bee for let-a-bee, like the bairns o' Kelty.
The speaker will give as good as he gets. 'Let-a-bee for let-a-bee' generally signifies mutual forbearance, but the addition of the phrase 'like the bairns of Kelty' reverses the usual meaning.

I'll mak the mantle meet for the man.
I will pay according to how well you treat me.

I'll ne'er lout sae laigh, an' lift sae little.
I will never stoop so low for so little reward.

I'll pay you, and put naething in your pouch.
A warning that the speaker intends giving the listener a beating.

I'll put daur ahint the door, and do't.
I will carry out my threats.

I'll tell the bourd, but no the body.
A saying denoting discretion. I will tell the joke or story, but not reveal the person involved.

I'm as auld as your auncient.
I am as wise as you think yourself. I will outwit you.

I'm forejidged, forefoughten, and forejeskit.
An alliterative expression denoting extreme fatigue.

I'm neither sma' drink thirsty, nor grey bread hungry.
Said when a person is offended by not receiving the hospitality that they had expected.

I'm no sae blind as I'm bleer-e'ed.
I am not so much blind as unwilling to see.

I'm speaking o' hay and you o' horse corn.
We are speaking about different things.

In a frost a nail is worth the horse.
Because it will give the horse some grip and hence may save it from falling and killing itself. Hence a small thing of no great importance may, at an opportune moment, be of great service.

I ne'er lo'ed water in my shoon, and my wame's made o' better leather.
Said by someone when they are offered a glass of water, but crave something a little stronger!

I ne'er sat on your coat tail.
I never impeded you in any way.

It doesna set a sow to wear a saddle.
It does not suit vulgar people to wear fine clothes.

Ither folk are weel saur'd, but ye're no sae vera.
Said in jest meaning that the person so addressed is no oil painting. To be 'weel saur'd' is to be good looking.

It maun e'en be ower shoon ower boots wi' me now.
Said by a person who has gone so far in a matter that they must go through with it come what may.

It's a far cry to Loch Awe.
Said when a person considers it safe to behave unlawfully because they are so far away from the seat of authority. This saying originates from a renegade member of the Clan Campbell, whose seat of power was at Loch Awe.

It's a gude tongue that says nae ill, but a better heart that thinks nane.

It's a lamb at the up-takin', but an auld sheep or ye get it aff.
A warning to those starting any habit which is addictive – it's easy to start but very difficult to stop later on.

It's an ill bird that files its ain nest.
It takes a truly bad person to harm his own kith and kin.

It's a sair time when the mouse looks out o' the meal barrel wi' a saut tear in its e'e.
Things are in a very sorry state when even the mice cannot find enough to eat.

It's a sin to lee on the deil.
You should always speak the truth, even of the worst people.

It's a sour reek when the gudewife dings the gudeman.
This proverb originates from a country tale of husband battering. A man seen coming out of his house with tears on his cheeks initially said that they were caused by smoke in the house, but on further enquiry admitted that his wife had beaten him.

It is better to travel hopefully than to arrive.
From *Virginibus Puerisque* (1881), by Robert Louis Stevenson.

It's by the mouth o' the cow that the milk comes.
You only get out what you put in to begin with.

It's drink will you, but no drink shall you.
A criticism of a person's hospitality, when they politely ask if you would like a drink, but press the matter no further.

It's growing to the grand, like a stirk's tail.
Meaning that something is not progressing in the desired direction.

It's gude to be sib to siller.
It is good to be related to wealthy persons.

It's gude to hae your cog out when it rains kail.
Make the most of your opportunities.

It's hard for a greedy e'e to hae a leal heart.
It is hard for a covetous person to be loyal and honest.

It's ill meddling between the bark and the rind.
It's better not to interfere between husband and wife, or close relations.

It's ill praising green barley.
It is not wise to praise things of which we are not sure how they will turn out.

It's ill speaking between a fu' man and a fasting.
A hungry man and a well-fed man are not usually on good terms with each other. This saying is sometimes used to encourage a guest to have something to eat. It was first recorded by Fergusson in his *Scottish Proverbs* around 1641.

It's ill to be ca'd a thief, and aye found picking.
It is not helpful to be found in suspicious circumstances if one already has a bad name.

It's ill to tak the breeks aff a Hielandman.
Highlanders proper were not in the habit of wearing anything under their kilts. Hence it is difficult to take from someone what they do not possess!

It's lang or four bare legs gather heat in a bed.
This saying is applied to young people who get married before they have everything necessary to support a successful marriage, thinking that love will be enough.

It's lang or the deil dees at the dike side.
It will be a long time before we hear of the death of someone who is a thorn in our flesh.

It's nae mair pity to see a woman greet than to see a goose go barefit.
A rather ungallant suggestion alluding to the facility with which women can avail themselves of tears to carry a point.

It's no the rumblin' cart that fa's first ower the brae.
It is not always the oldest or most infirm person who dies first.

It's no tint, a friend gets.
We all benefit when a friend gets something.

It's stinking praise comes out o' ane's ain mouth.
Self praise is no praise at all.

It stoors in an oor.
A Lanarkshire farming expression to describe the dryness of the soil, i.e. it turns to dust quickly.

It was ne'er a gude aiver that flung at the broose.
More words of warning to those contemplating marriage. If there is trouble at the outset, things are unlikely to go smoothly thereafter. The 'broose' was a race held at country weddings.

It will aye be a dirty dub between them.
It will always be a point of contention between them.

It will be the last word o' his testament.
He will delay from doing a thing for as long as possible.

It will mak a braw show in a landward kirk.
Said by somebody when their opinion is asked of something which they consider vulgar or gaudy.

It would be a hard task to follow a black dockit sow through a burnt muir this night.
It's pitch black.

It would be a pity to hae spoilt twa houses wi' them.
Spoken when two disagreeable people get married to each other.

'I winna mak a toil o' a pleasure', quo' the man when he buried his wife.

I winna mak fish o' ane an' flesh o' anither.
I will show no favours but treat all alike.

I wouldna be deaved wi' your keckling for a' your eggs.
Your bad points outweigh your good ones.

I wouldna hae kent ye if I had met ye in my parritch.
I wouldn't recognise you even if we came face to face.

I would rather be your Bible than your horse.
A humorous allusion to the fact that the subject neglects the former and overworks the latter.

I would rather my bannock burn than that you should turn't.
I would rather suffer than be indebted to you in any way.

Jeddart justice – first hang a man and syne try him.

Jock's a mislear'd imp, but ye're a rum-deil.
Jock may be mischievious but he's well behaved by your standards.

Jouk, and let the jaw gang by.
Literally, duck and let the deluge pass by. It is better to yield to the inevitable and wait until it has passed.

'Just as it fa's', quo the wooer to the maid.
Legend has it that when a courtier went to woo a maid she was preparing the meal and had a drop at the end of her nose. When she asked him if he was going to stay the night he replied as above, meaning that if the drop fell into his meat he would leave, and if not he would stay.

Kame sindle, kame sair.
Literally, if the hair is seldom combed it becomes tangled and hence painful to comb, i.e. if we don't carry out routine chores, we are storing up trouble for the future.

Kamesters are aye creeshy.
People are always like their work.

Katie Sweerock, frae where she sat, cried, 'Reik me this, and reik me that.'
A saying applied to lazy people who get others to carry out chores they should be doing themselves.

Keek in the stoup, was ne'er a gude fellow.
Said of one who looks into the pot to see if the drink is nearly finished rather than drinking up and ordering more when his glass is empty.

Keep a thing seven years and ye'll find a use for't.
The hoarder's motto.

Keep out o' his company that cracks o' his cheatery.
Do not become associated with a person who boasts of his cunning.

Keep something for a sair fit.
Keep something for a rainy day.

Keep woo, and it will be dirt, keep lint, and it will be silk.
Lint improves with keeping, but wool deteriorates.

Keep your ain fish guts to your ain sea-maws.
Keep any extras which you may accrue for your own kith and kin rather than for others. Charity begins at home.

Keep your ain grease for your ain cart wheels.
Of similar sentiments to the preceding proverb.

Keep your breath to cool your parritch.
Said to people who have let off steam in a moment of anger.

Keep your gab steekit when ye kenna you company.
Be silent when you are in the company of strangers.

Keep your mouth shut and your een open.

Ken when to spend and when to spare, and ye needna be busy, and ye'll ne'er be bare.
Advice on how to live happily within one's means.

Kindle a candle at baith ends and it'll soon be done.

Kings are kittle cattle to shoe behint.
Kings are not to be trusted.

King's cauff's worth ither men's corn.
Even the little benefits which attend the King's service are worth more than most men's wages. This saying was recorded in Carmichaell's *Proverbs in Scots* around 1628, and is quoted in the writings of both Burns and Scott.

King's cheese gaes half away in parings.
A large part of a King's income is absorbed in the expense of collecting it.

Kissing is cried down since the shaking o' hands.
In the 1720s the Church made a proclamation forbidding all
kissing by the mouth. Hand shaking however was allowed.
This saying was spoken by women who were asked for a kiss
but who were unwilling to allow it.

Kiss my foot, there's mair flesh on't.
A reply to those who try to ingratiate themselves by asking
permission to kiss the hand.

Kythe in your ain colours, that folk may ken ye.

Lacking breeds laziness, but praise breeds pith.
Positive comment will spur somebody on, negative comment
the reverse.

Laith to drink, laith frae't.
Although some people are slow to take to something, once
started it can be difficult to get them to stop.

Lang and sma', gude for naething ava.
A cheeky remark about tall thin people.

Lang ere the deil dee by the dyke-side.
Said when the improbable death of an ill disposed but
powerful person is talked of.

Lang mint, little dint.
'Much ado about nothing'.

Lang-tongued wives gang lang wi' bairn.
Said of people who broadcast their plans long before they are
sure they will be completed.

**Lassies are like lamb legs, they'll neither saut nor
keep.**
Enjoy yourself while you're young.

Law-makers shouldna be law-breakers.
Those laying down the rules cannot afford to set a bad
example.

Lay your wame to your winning.
Make sure you balance your consumption with your earnings.

Lean on the brose ye got in the morning.
Said facetiously to a person who leans heavily upon others.

Learn young, learn fair; learn auld, learn mair.

Learn your gudewife to mak milk kail.
The equivalent of 'teach your grandmother to suck eggs'.

Learn you an ill habit and ye'll ca't custom.
Said to people one suspects of taking advantage.

Leave aff while the play's gude.
Quit while the going is good.

Leave welcome aye behint you.
Don't outstay your welcome.

Leears should hae gude memories.
If they don't want to be caught out!

Let alane mak's mony lurden.
Want of correction makes a bad fellow. Spare the rod and spoil the child.

Let aye the bell'd wether break the snaw.
A 'bell'd wether' is the oldest and most experienced ram in the flock which wears a bell round its neck. Hence, when undertaking a difficult or dangerous task, one should let the most experienced go first.

Let him tak' a spring on his ain fiddle.
Said of a foolish or an unreasonable person, as if to say 'For the present we will allow him to have his own way.' Walter Scott's Bailie Nicol Jarvie quotes the proverb with great bitterness when he warns his opponent that his triumph will come before long: 'A weel, aweel, sir; you're welcome to a tune on your ain fiddle; But see if I dinna gar ye dance till't afore it's dune.'

Let ilka ane ruse the ford as they find it.
Let everyone speak of a thing as they find it.

Let na the plough stand to kill a mouse.
Do not neglect important duties for the sake of smaller matters.

Let ne'er your gear owergang ye.
Never let wealth make you forget your old friends.

Let the eird bear the dike.
Important undertakings should have a solid foundation.

Let the horns gang wi' the hide.
Throw in the extras free of charge to the purchaser.

Let the kirk stand i' the kirk yard.
Let everything be in its proper place.

'Lights heartsome', quo' the thief to the Lammas mune.
Before battery torches, robbers used to go thieving by moonlight.

Liked gear is half-bought.
Once you have set your heart on something it is difficult not to purchase it.

Like hens, ye rin aye to the heap.
A humorous tease spoken to those who help themselves to what there is most of on the table.

Likely lies i' the mire, and unlikely gets ower.
Meaning that many promising undertakings fail, whereas those which at first look less promising are successfully carried through.

Like Orkney butter, neither gude to eat nor creesh woo.
Said of something which has no use whatsoever.

Like the cur in the crab, he'll neither do nor let do.
A Scottish version of 'dog in a manger'.

Like the wabster, stealing through the warld.
A reply to an enquiry as to how one is getting on. Again, another insult to the weaving profession.

Like the wife that ne'er cries for the ladle till the pat rins o'er.
Said of one who never asks until it is too late.

Lips gae, laps gae, drink and pay.
If you put a drink to your lips be prepared to put your hand to your lap to take out your purse.

Little Jock gets the little dish, and that hauds him lang little.
The poorest get the least, which ensures they remain the poorest.

Little kens the auld wife, as she sits by the fire, what the wind is doing on Hurley-Burley-Swire.
A warning to armchair critics that they cannot possibly know the trouble faced by others. The 'Hurley Burley Swire' is a passage through a ridge of mountains that separate Nithsdale from Tweeddale and Clydesdale, and there is a perpetual wind forced through this gap.

Little mense o' the cheeks to bite aff the nose.
It is silly for a person to injure another on whom they depend in some way.

Little wit in the head maks muckle travel to the feet.
People not blessed with much sense are apt to be sent on fools' errands.

Loud coos the doo when the hawk's no whistling, loud cheeps the mouse when the cat's no rustling.
When the cat's away, the mice will play.

Loud i' the loan was ne'er a gude milk cow.
According to Kelly this saying was used as a reprimand to noisy girls. Empty vessels make the loudest noise.

Love is as warm amang cottars as courtiers.
Love knows no bounds.

Maidens should be mim till they're married, and then they may burn the kirks.
Anything goes, but only once you're married.

Maidens' tochers and ministers' stipends are aye less than ca'd.

Maidens want naething but a man, and then they want a'thing.
Clearly this saying was conceived before the women's movement existed.

Mair by luck than gude guiding.
Said when a person's good fortune is due to luck rather than personal merit.

'Mair whistle than woo,' quo' the souter when he sheared the sow.

Maister's will is gude wark.
The reason for this is that the master is sure to be pleased with it.

Mak a kirk or a mill o't.
Make what you please of it.

Mak nae toom ruse.
Don't give empty praise.

Man proposes, God disposes.

Man's twal is no sae gude as the deil's dizzen.
'Man's twal' is only twelve whereas the 'deil's dizzen' is thirteen.

March dust and May sun, mak corn white and maidens dun.

Married folk are like rats in a trap – fain to get ithers in, but fain to get out themsels.

Marry abune your match, and get a maister.
Marry someone from a higher social standing and they will lord it over you.

Maun do is a fell fallow.
Necessity is a hard master.

Maybe your pat may need my clips.
Perhaps you will be glad of my assistance some day, even if you do not welcome it now.

May birds are aye cheeping.
This proverb relates to the proverb that it is unlucky to marry in May, as the offspring of such marriages are said to die.

May he that turns the clod ne'er want a bannock.
May the hardworking never go hungry.

Mealy mou'd maidens stand lang at the mill.

Measure twice, cut but ance.
If you prepare things properly you will only have to do them once.

Meat and mass never hindered man.

Meat feeds, claith deeds, but breeding maks the man.

Misterfu' folk maunna be mensefu.
Beggars should not be choosers.

Mist in May and heat in June make the harvest right soon.

Mist on the hills, weather spills; Mist i' the howes, weather growes.
A Fife weather forecasting rhyme.

Mistress before folk, gudewife behint backs: whaur lies the dishclout?
A saying applied in jest to those who are very particular in their manner of speaking.

Money is like the muck midden, it does nae gude till it be spread.

Mony a gude tale is spoilt in the telling.

Mony a little maks a mickle or Mony littles mak a muckle.
Lots of little things can make a great thing. Often erroneously quoted as 'Mony a mickle maks a muckle.' 'Muckle' is merely a variant of the word 'mickle', both meaning a large quantity or amount.

Mony ane for land taks a fool by the hand.
Many only marry for material wealth.

Mony ane kens the gude fellow that disna ken the gudewife.
The reason for this is that some men are only 'gudefellows' when they escape their domestic environments for the company of the local hostelry.

Mony ane kisses the bairn for love o' the nurse.
Many show kindness to the friends and relations upon whom
they have designs in the hope of attracting their good
opinion.

**Mony ane maks an errand to the ha' to bid my leddy
good day.**
Many occupy their lives with trifles.

Mony a thing's made for the pennie.
Many contrivances are thought of to get money.

Mony a true tale's tauld in jest.
This saying is recorded in Carmichaell's *Proverbs in Scots* as
'Manie suith word said in bourding.'

Mony aunts, mony emes, mony kin, but few friends.
A person may have many relations, but few friends among
them.

Mony care for meal that hae baked bread enough.
Some people will still complain even when they have enough
to eat themselves.

Mony haws, mony snaws.
A piece of long-range weather forecasting supposedly
connecting a large harvest of berries with a bad winter to
follow.

Mony wyte their wife for their ain thriftless life.
Many people blame others for the consequences of their own
actions.

Moyen does muckle, but money does mair.
Influence does much, but money is even more effective.

Muckle gude may it do you, and merry go doun, every lump as big as my thoom.
A nasty wish – that every mouthful may choke you.

Muckle spoken, part spilt.
A saying applied when so much has been said on a topic that a lot of it has been lost.

Muckle wad aye hae mair.
Those who have a lot always want more.

Naebody is riving your claes to get you.
Nobody is unduly bothered about you.

Nae butter will stick to my bread.
I am unlucky.

Nae equal to you but our dog Sorkie, and he's dead so ye're marrowless.
Said sarcastically to boastful people.

Nae faut; but she set her bannet ower weel.
The only fault is that she is too good looking.

Nae faut that the cat has a clean band, she sets a bannet sae weel.
Said ironically to people who pretend to do, have, or wear something that does not become them.

Nae gairdner ever lichtlied his ain leeks.
No person will speak ill of what they value dearly.

Nae gain without pain.
Nothing comes easily.

Nae man can baith sup and blaw at ance.
No one can do two opposing things at once.

Nae man can live langer in peace than his neighbours like.
Good neighbours should be cherished.

Nae man can seek his marrow i' the kirn sae weel as him that has been in't himsel.
It takes one to know one.

Nae sooner up than her head's in the aumrie.
Applied to greedy people, implying that they are no sooner out of bed than they think of their stomachs and go looking for food in the cupboard.

Naething comes fairer to light than what has been lang hidden.
One gets great pleasure from finding something which has been lost for a long time.

Naething is got without pains but an ill name and lang nails.

Naething like being stark dead.
There is nothing like doing something thoroughly. A malicious proverb said to have been used on hearing of the death of an enemy.

Naething sae bauld as a blind mear.
Ignorance can breed confidence.

Naething sooner maks a man auld-like than fitting ill to his meat.
Nothing ages a person faster than being ill fed.

Naething to be done in haste but gripping fleas.
A cautionary proverb to think things through first.

Naething to do but draw in your stool and sit down.
Said when all preliminaries have already been taken care of
and only the finishing touch is needed. Often applied to a
courting man, when all that is left is for him to actually
propose.

Nae wonder ye're auld like, ilka thing fashes you.

Nane can mak a bore but ye'll find a pin for't.
None can criticise you, but you will find an excuse.

Nane can tell what's i' the shaup till it's shelt.
You can't judge from outward appearances alone.

Nearest the heart nearest the mou.
A saying applied when someone meaning to name one
person, by mistake names another – perhaps a sweetheart,
and hence betrays what is on their mind.

Nearest the king nearest the widdy.
People who support the King should be careful what they
say, as they only hold their positions at his pleasure.

Near's my sark, but nearer's my skin.
Some people are closer to me than others, but at the end of
the day I am closest to myself.

Near the kirk, but far frae grace.

Neck or naething, the king lo'es nae cripples.
This saying is a wish that should someone be in an accident,
that they either break their neck or escape injury completely,
because any disability will render them useless.

**Ne'er break out o' kind to gar your friends ferlie at
you.**
Do not act out of character merely to astonish your friends.

Ne'er do ill that gude may come o't.
Be careful. The end does not always justify the means.

Ne'er draw your dirk when a dunt will do.
Don't resort to extreme measures when they are not
necessary.

Ne'er fash your thoom.
Don't trouble yourself.

**Ne'er find faut wi' my shoon, unless you pay my
souter.**
A rebuke to those who criticise somebody's appearance.

Ne'er gie me death in a toom dish.
A joke said by persons who like their food, i.e. if you are
going to kill me, please do not do it by starvation – give me
food.

**Ne'er lippen ower muckle to a new friend or an auld
enemy.**

Ne'er misca' a Gordon in the raws o' Strathbogie.
Never speak badly of somebody on their home territory. The
Gordons were the ruling clan in Strathbogie.

**Ne'er put your hand farther out than your sleeve will
reach.**
Don't overstretch your resources.

Ne'er use the taws when a gloom will do.
Don't resort to extreme measures when they are not
necessary.

Next to nae wife, a gude wife is the best.
More Caledonian misogyny.

Nipping and scarring's Scotch folk's wooing.

O' a' meat i' the warld, the drink gaes best doon.

O' a' sorrow, a fu' sorrow's the best.
Traditionally said when friends die and leave good legacies.

O' bairns' gifts ne'er be fain; nae sooner they gie than they tak it again.

O' ill debtors men get aiths.
All you will get from a debtor is a promise rather than the money itself.

On painting and fighting look adreich.
When observing a painting or a fight, it is best to look from a distance. Sound advice.

Open confession is gude for the soul.
This proverb is recorded in Fergusson's *Scottish Proverbs*, and hence must predate 1641.

Oppression will mak a wise man wud.

Our sins and debts are aften mair than we think.
A cautionary saying.

Out o' Davy Lindsay into Wallace.
Said when a person has progressed from one thing to another. David Lindsay and Wallace were two books formerly used in schools.

Out o' the peat pot into the gutter.
A Scottish equivalent of the English 'Out of the frying pan and into the fire'.

Out o' the warld and into Kippen.
At one time Kippen was considered to be so remote that it was out of this world. The proverb is used when a person is going to a strange unknown place.

O, wad some power the giftie gie us To see oursels as ithers see us!
From Robert Burns' poem 'To a louse'.

Ower braw a purse to put a plack in.
Said when somebody builds a grand house on a small income.

Ower high, ower laigh, ower het, ower cauld.
Said when someone or thing goes from one extreme to the other.

Ower mony cooks spoil the broth.

Ower mony grieves hinder the wark.

Ower mony irons in the fire, some maun cool.
Said when somebody has so many projects on the go at once, that they are unlikely to make a success of them all.

Ower muckle hameliness spoils gude courtesy.
Familiarity breeds contempt.

Ower muckle loose leather about your chafts.
A somewhat unsubtle, but marvellously expressive way of saying that a person is not looking well, or too thin.

Ower muckle o' ae thing is gude for naething.

Ower narrow counting culyes nae kindness.
Meanness does not cultivate kindness from others.

Ower sicker, ower loose.
A saying applied to someone who is either too strict and hard, or too free and easy.

Patch and lang sit, build and soon flit.
A long gradual rise is more likely to be permanent than a
rapid one.

Pay-before-hand's never weel ser'd.
Tradesmen suffer equally from two types of customer –
those who never pay, and those who pay before the job is
done and hence never stop acting as foremen.

Penny-wheep's gude enough for muslin-kail.
Penny wheep was the weakest kind of small beer sold for a
penny a bottle and muslin kail is a common kind of broth.
Hence poor service deserves nothing better than a poor
reward.

Penny wise and pound foolish.

Peter's in, Paul's out.
Said when, after waiting an age for a principal character to
arrive, another principal leaves on his arrival.

Pigs may whistle, but they hae an ill mouth for't.
Said when somebody is trying to perform a task for which
they are incompetent.

Pint stoups hae lang lugs.
This saying arises because those who drink a lot often say
more than is good for them.

Play carle wi' me again if you daur.
Do not dare to argue with me. Often said by parents to
stubborn children.

**Pleaing at the law is like fighting through a whin bush
– the harder the blows the sairer the scarts.**
A comment on the difficult process of law and the state it is
likely to leave you in.

**Poor folk seek meat for their stamacks, and rich folk
stamacks for their meat.**

Poortith's pain, but nae disgrace.
Poverty is uncomfortable, but nothing to be ashamed of.

Praise without profit puts little i' the pat.
Fine words do not put food in one's stomach.

Pride an' sweerdness need muckle uphaudin.

Puddins and paramours should be hetly handled.
Both are not so pleasant when cold!

Put a coward to his metal, and he'll fight the deil.
Once roused, people can find incredible courage.

**Put anither man's bairn in your bosom and he'll creep
oot at your sleeve.**
You cannot expect to be loved just because you look after
someone.

Put your finger in the fire, and say it was your fortune.
Said of a person who has knowingly placed themself in
difficulties, but who attributes their position to fortune.

Put your hand twice to your bannet and ance to your pouch.
A piece of advice hinting that the more polite one is the less often one has to pay.

Put your shanks in your thanks and mak gude gramashes o' them.
Literally this says 'put your legs in your thanks and make good gaiters of them.' A rebuke to those who pay in thanks only.

Put your thoom upon that.
Keep it secret.

Quality without quantity is little thought o'.

Quey calves are dear veal.
A quey is a two-year-old cow, and hence too valuable as a
cow to be killed as a calf.

Quick at meat, quick at wark.

Quick, for you'll ne'er be cleanly.
Do something quickly, for you will never do it neatly.

Quick returns mak rich merchants.

Quietness is best.
Silence is golden.

Raggit folk and bonny folk are aye ta'en haud o'.
Said as a joke when somebody catches or tears their clothing on a nail.

Raise nae mair deils than ye are able to lay.
Don't take on more tasks than you can handle.

Rather spoil your joke than tine your friend.
Do not tell jokes if it is at the expense of a friend, as their friendship is worth a lot more than a laugh.

Rattan an' moose
Lea' the poor woman's hoose;
Gang awa ower to the mill.
And there ane and a' ye'll get your fill.
This verse was written on the walls by those whose dwellings were vermin-infested, in the hope of them leaving the premises.

Raw dads mak fat lads.
Presumably because they are not experienced enough to get work out of them.

Reavers shouldna be ruers.
A person should not be a robber if he has a conscience and wants to repent.

Reckless youth maks ruefu' eild.
You can be sure that the past will catch you up.

Remember, man, and keep in mind, a faithfu' friend is hard to find.

Remove an auld tree an' it'll wither.

Riches are got wi' pain, kept wi' care, and tint wi' grief.
A proverb pointing out the hardships associated with wealth.

Rich folk hae routh o' friends.
Money attracts many 'friends'.

Right, Roger, sow's gude mutton.
Said when somebody is completely mistaken.

Right wrangs nae man.

Rise when the day daws, bed when the night fa's.

Ruse the fair day at e'en.
Don't give praise until a thing is complete.

Ruse the ford as ye find it.
Speak as you find.

Rusted wi' eild, a wee piece gate seems lang.
The ravages of time can make a short road seem much longer.

Sair cravers are aye ill payers.
And vice versa.

Sairs shouldna be sair handled.
One should handle delicate matters gently.

Sairy be your meal-pock, and aye your nieve i' the neuk o't.
An ill wish that someone's meal bag will be empty when they next delve in to get some food.

'Saut' quo the souter, when he had eaten a cow a' but the tail.
These words are used to spur on those who are beginning to tire when they have almost completed a difficult task.

Save yoursel frae the deil and the laird's bairns.
A warning given by poor people, in days gone by, to their children. It was well known that if they hurt the laird's children they would be punished, but if it were the other way round, nothing could be done.

Say aye 'No', and ye'll ne'er be married.
A humorous remark made to someone who has just refused some offer.

Say wee! and dae weel, and wi' ae letter; say weel is gude, but dae weel is better.

Scant-o'-grace hears lang preachings.

Scart-the-cog wad sup mair.
To 'scart the cog' is to scrape the inside of the dish, hence suggesting that the contents have been so popular, a little more would not go amiss.

Scorn comes commonly wi' skaith.

Scotsmen aye reckon frae an ill hour.

Scotsmen aye tak their mark frae a mischief.
The above proverb and the preceding one are both comments on the less positive side of the Scottish character. It is said that Scotsmen tend to calculate things in relation to the date of some mishap or death. This is the silliest notion I have come across since my last car accident.

Seek muckle, and get something; seek little, and get naething.
It pays to set one's sights high.

Seldom ride tines his spurs.
If you don't use it, you can lose it.

Sel, sel, has half-filled hell.
Selfishness has caused grief for many people.

Send your gentle blude to the market, and see what it will buy.
Said to those who boast of coming from a high-ranking family, but who possess little else.

Send you to the sea, and ye'll no get saut water.
Said when somebody does not live up to your expectations.

Set a stout heart to a stey brae.
Face a hard task with courage and determination. This
saying is recorded in Alexander Montgomerie's famous
poem 'The Cherrie and the Slae', first published in 1597
thus: 'So gets ay, that sets ay, Stout stomackis to the brae.'

Set that doun on the backside o' your count book.
Take note of my help, and make sure you repay it in the
future.

Shak yer ain mats at yer ain back door.
Attend to your own life and let others attend to theirs.

Shallow waters mak maist din.
Another version of empty vessels making the loudest noise.

She brak her elbow at the kirk door.
Said of a woman who becomes lazy when she marries.

**She hauds up her gab like an awmous dish. She hauds
up her head like a hen drinking water.**
Both of the above sayings are used on people who behave in
an impudent or forward manner.

**She'll keep her ain side of the house, and gang up and
down yours.**
A saying used to dissuade a man from marrying a woman
who is considered to be too bold and pushy. It is a warning
that she will take over everything in his life.

She lookit at the moon, but lichtit i' the midden.
An old proverb applied to women who boast before marriage
that they will find a 'fine' match, but who afterwards end up
marrying ordinary men.

She looks like a leddy in a landward kirk.
A saying applied to someone who appears highly
conspicuous on account of their dress or manner.

She pined awa' like Jenkin's hen.
She died an old maid.

She's a wise wife that wats her ain weird.
She is a clever wife who knows her own destiny.

She's black, but she has a sweet smack.
Wealthy but not very beautiful – for those who would marry only for money.

She that fa's ower a strae's a tentless taupie.
The person who falls at the smallest of obstacles is a fool.

Shod i' the cradle, and barefit i' the stubble.
Applied to people who dress inappropriately.

Sic as ye gie, sic will you get.
You only get out of life what you put in.

Sic things maun be if we sell ale.
According to Kelly, this was the reply an innkeeper's wife gave when her husband complained that the visiting exciseman was being too familiar with her.

Sit down and rest you, and tell us how they drest you, and how you wan awa.
A humorous way of asking a person about people they have been visiting.

Snailie, snailie, shoot oot yer horn,
And tell us if it'll be a bonny day the morn.
A popular rhyme with country children at one time, eager to forecast the next day's weather.

Sodgers, fire, and water soon mak room for themsels.
One has little control over any of these. This saying clearly dates from the time when accommodation could be seized to billet soldiers in.

Some are gey drouthy, but ye're aye moistified.
An insinuation that a person likes their drink.

Some fork low, but ye fork ower the mow.
Some people do not work hard enough, but you overdo it.

Some hae a hantel o' fauts, ye're only a ne'er-do-weel.
Some people, although badly behaved, have some redeeming qualities, the person thus addressed has none.

Some hae meat that canna eat,
And some wad eat that want it;
But we hae meat, and we can eat,
For which the Lord be thankit.
This verse is generally known as the Selkirk Grace. Robert Burns may have repeated it at Lord Selkirk's table, but the probability is that it was current at the time among the peasantry.

Some say the Deil's deid an buried in Kirkcaldy.

Some that has the least to dree are loudest wi' 'waes me'.
It is often those who suffer least who complain the most.

Sorrow an' ill weather come unca'd.
Both are beyond our control.

Souters and tailors, count hours.
Tradesmen and those involved in commerce are aware of the value of time.

Speak o' the deil and he'll appear.
A humorous remark made when the subject of a conversation suddenly appears.

Speak when ye're spoken to; do what ye're bidden; come when ye're ca'd, and ye'll no be chidden.
A strong remark used as a rebuke when somebody joins in a conversation without waiting to be invited to do so.

Stay and drink o' your ain broust.
Wait and join in the mischief which you have caused.

Stuffing hauds out storms.
Advice to eat well before undertaking a journey in bad weather.

Sturt pays nae debt.
Said to people who fly into a rage when asked to pay what they are due.

Sweet at the on-taking, but soor in the aff-putting.
An allusion to the contracting of debt, or some other liability.

Tak a hair o' the dog that bit you.
A familiar version of the law of Homeopathy *(Similia similibus curantur)*, which is usually interpreted by drinkers thus – cure your hangover by taking another glass.

Tak a piece; your teeth's langer than your beard.
Said to children to encourage them to take an extra titbit when it is offered.

Tak awa Aberdeen and twal mile round and far are ye?
Aberdonians tend to think that the north of Scotland would be nothing without it. I couldn't agree more!

Tak your ain will o't, as the cat did o' the haggis – first ate it, and then creepit into the bag.
Said to people who persist in carrying out an unreasonable act.

Tak your meal wi' ye an' your brose will be the thicker.
A saying sarcastically applied by those who indulge in a good meal before they go to have one with a friend, signifying that they do not expect to be overly well fed there.

Taury breeks pays nae freight.
People who are in the same line of business can usually expect perks from each other.

That bolt came ne'er out o' your bag.
The thing is better done/told than you could do it.

That'll be a sap out o' my bicker.
That is bad news as it will reduce my income.

That's abune your thoom.
Said to a person who is about to do something of which he is thought to be incapable.

That's as ill as the ewes in the yaird and nae dogs to hunt them.
That is quite right.

That's for the faither, and no for the son.
A saying used when a job has been done on the cheap, and hence is unlikely to last more than one generation.

That's the way to marry me if ere you should hap to do it.
A sharp rebuke to those who presume to be too familiar.

That which God will gie the deil canna reeve.
Said when a person has attained their goal in spite of opposition.

That will be when the deil's blind, an' he's no bleer-e'ed yet.
That will never happen.

The best laid schemes o' mice and men gang aft agley.
I.e. often go awry. Taken from Robert Burns' *Poems* (1786).

The better day the better deed.
The humorous answer given by someone who is accused or blamed for doing something on a Sunday.

The bird maun flichter that flees with a'e wing.
This proverb is often used to justify having a further treat, especially a drink.

The breath o' a fause friend's waur than the fuff o' a weasel.
Fuffing is the frightening sound made by a weasel before it attacks, but even this is not considered as awful as the breath of a deceitful friend.

The cow may want her tail yet.
Said as a warning to people that they might need your kindness later, even though they deny you theirs just now.

The cow that's first up gets the first o' the dew.
Another version of 'It's the early bird that catches the worm.' This saying is used as an incentive to be up and working early.

The day has een, the night has lugs.
A warning to be cautious at all times.

The day you do weel there will be seven munes in the lift and ane on the midden.
It would appear highly unlikely that the person so addressed will ever do anything well.

The deil doesna aye show his cloven cloots.
Evil things and people can come in disguise.

The deil's a busy bishop in his ain diocie.
You can be sure that bad people will be active in promoting their own bad ends.

The deil's aye gude to his ain.
Originally meant in all seriousness, this saying is now usually used in jest. It was believed that the devil had the power to provide for his followers.

The deil's bairns hae deil's luck.
Spoken enviously when bad people prosper.

The deil's nae sae ill as he's ca'ed.
Most people may be found to have some redeeming feature.

The deil's pet lambs lo'e Claverse's lads.
A saying dating back to the Covenanters, claiming that the
followers of Graham of Claverhouse were on intimate terms
with the devil.

**The deil was sick, the deil a monk wad be; the deil
grew hale, syne deil a monk was he.**
A warning that promises that they will change their ways
made by those on their sick beds are seldom kept on
recovery.

The e'ening brings a' hame.
The twilight years and approach of death softens many
people's political and religious differences.

**The Englishman greets, the Irishman sleeps, but the
Scotchman gangs till he gets it.**
A saying purporting to give an account of the behaviour of
these three nations when they want meat.

The fat sow's tail's aye creeshed.
Those who already have plenty are always getting additions
to their stores.

The fish that sooms in a dub will aye taste o' mud.
You can never change your upbringing.

**The grandsire buys, the faither bigs, the son sells, and
the grandson thigs.**
Literally this saying says that the grandfather buys the estate,
the father builds upon it, the son sells the property, and
forces the grandson in turn to beg. The saying is alluding to
the uncertainty of worldly goods, and the fate which can
befall family fortunes.

The gravest fish is an oyster;
The gravest bird's an ool;
The gravest beast's an ass;
And the gravest man's a fool.

The gude or ill hap o' a gude or ill life is the gude or ill choice o' a gude or ill wife.
The man who has a good wife can bear any ill fortune, whereas the man who chooses his wife unwisely can expect no happiness in life.

The king lies doun, yet the warld rins round.
The world does not stop just because the King lies down, i.e. no one is indispensable.

The king may come in the cadger's gait.
Beware – those you offend may in the future return in a superior position.

The kirk is muckle, but ye may say mass in ae end o't.

The loudest hummer's no the best bee.

The man may eithly tine a stot that canna count his kine.
The person who does not know what he is doing cannot be expected to look after his own business.

**The men o' the East
Are pykin their geese,
And sendin' their feathers here-awa there-awa.**
An old rhyme said by children when it started to snow.

The men o' the Mearns manna do mair than they may.
Even the men of Kincardineshire can only do their utmost – a proverb intended to be complimentary to the men of that county.

The mother of mischief is no bigger than a midge's wing.

Them that herd swine, aye hear them gruntin'.

The nearer e'en the mair beggars.
A humorous welcome given to people who drop in to visit a friend.

The next time ye dance, ken wha ye tak by the hand.
A warning to those who have imprudently got involved with people who were too cunning for them in the past, to take more care in choosing their friends.

The nights fair draw in, after the Brig O' Allan Games.
A local saying commenting on the approach of dark winter nights.

The piper wants muckle that wants the nether chaft.
An expression used when some necessary part is found to be wanting.

The poor man pays for a'.
He pays for the rich through his labours and he pays for himself with his wages.

The proof o' a pudding's the preein' o't.
The proof of the pudding is in the tasting, i.e. you cannot pass judgement until you have experienced something at first hand.

The proudest nettle grows on a midden.
The proudest of people have often come from very humble origins.

The rain comes scouth when the wind's in the south.
'Scouth' means freely or heavily in this sense.

There are mair maidens than maukins.
Used to console a man when he has lost his girlfriend.

There are mair married than gude house hauders.
There are more people who qualify as householders than are competent for the duties of the position.

There are nane sae weel shod but may slip.
No person, no matter their wealth, is immune from mishap.

There belangs mair to a bed than four bare legs.
More advice for the couple intending to marry, warning them that there are many hidden costs.

There ne'er came ill frae a gude advice.

There ne'er was a five pound note but there was a ten pound road for't.
No matter how much money we have it never seems to be enough, as we instantly raise our sights even higher.

There's a dub at every door, and before some doors there's twa.
Every household has a skeleton in its cupboard, and some more than one.

There's a measure in a' things, even in kail supping.
There is a reason for everything.

There's an act in the Laird o' Grant's court, that no abune eleven speak at ance.
A humorous remark made when too many people try to speak at once.

There's a reason for ye, an' a rag about the foot o't.
Spoken when the reason given for doing something would appear to be a lame one.

There's as mony Johnstones as Jardines.
There is an equal chance.

There's a whaup i' the raip.
There is a knot in the rope, i.e. there is something amiss.

There's a word in my wame, but it's ower far down.
An expression used by someone who cannot find the
appropriate word.

There's aye some water whaur the stirkie drowns.
There is no trouble without some cause.

**'There's baith meat and music here', quo the dog
when he ate the piper's bag.**

There's little for the rake after the shool.
There is not much to be had of a thing once greedy people
have been at it.

There's mair room without than within.
A remark made by a person who thinks that their company is
not wanted.

There's mair ways o' killing a dog than hanging him.
The same ends can be brought about in many different
ways.

There's mair whistling wi' you than gude red land.
'Red land' is ground turned over by the plough.
Hence the proverb is hinting that there is more play than
work.

There's muckle ado when dominies ride.
When people do something out of their ordinary sphere,
there must be some necessity for it.

There's nae great loss without some gain.

There's nae hawk flees sae high but he will stoop to some lure.
Every man has his price.

There's nae iron sae hard but rust will fret it; there's nae claith sae fine but moths will eat it.
Nothing lasts forever, no matter the quality.

There's ower mony nicks in your horn.
You are too cunning for me.

There's remedie for a' but stark dead.

There's twa enoughs, and ye hae gotten ane o' them.
The two enoughs are big enough and little enough. This saying is used as an answer to those who say that they have enough – meaning that the speaker has little enough.

There's twa things in my mind, and that's the least o' them.
Said when the speaker declines to give a reason for something which he does not wish to do.

There was ne'er a gude toun but there was a dub at the end o't.
Nothing is perfect.

There was mair lost at Sherramuir, whaur the Hielandman lost his faither, and his mither, and a gude buff belt worth baith o' them.
A remark made in jest when somebody has sustained a trifling loss.

The smith's mear and the souter's wife are aye warst shod.

The third time's lucky.

The thrift o' you and the woo o' a dog wad make a braw wab.
A sarcastic way of telling someone that they are lazy.

The tod ne'er sped better than when he gaed his ain errand.
Every man is most zealous when working for his own interest.

The water will ne'er waur the widdie.
Literally the water will never cheat the gallows. This is another version of the proverb 'He that's born to be hanged will never be drowned.'

The wife's aye welcome that comes wi' a crookit oxter.
The person carrying a present is always welcome, hence the 'crookit oxter'.

They are eith hindered that are no furdersome.
Those who are not keen are easily distracted from doing something.

They are lifeless wha're fautless.

They can fin' fauts wha canna mend them.

They may dunsh that gie the lunch.
This saying means that those upon whom we depend can do whatever they like with us. There is no accurate translation into English of the word 'dunsh', but it roughly means to jog or thrust in violent manner.

They may ken by your beard what has been on your board.
The remains of your last meal are stuck to your face, or your face will give away what you have been up to.

They ne'er gie wi' the spit but they gat wi' the ladle.
Said of people who never confer a small favour without expecting a large one in return.

They're aye gude will'd o' their horse that hae nane.
People are always willing to help who are not in a position to
do so.

They're fremit friends that canna be fash'd.
If they cannot be bothered to help, they are a strange sort of
friend.

They're no to be named in the same day.
The two things are totally different.

**They speak o' my drinking, but ne'er think o' my
drouth.**
Said when people complain about the actions of an
individual, without considering the causes of their behaviour.

They that rise wi' the sun hae their wark weel begun.

They that see but your head dinna see your height.
Said to people who are not physically very tall, but who have
high-spirited personalities.

**They that see you through the day winna break the
house for you at night.**
The person thus addressed is no oil painting in the beauty
stakes.

They were scant o' bairns that brought you up.
A saying applied to a very rude and bad-mannered person as
a rebuke.

**This and better may do, but this and waur will never
do.**
A suggestion that a thing has been badly done.

Three can keep a secret when twa are awa.
You can only trust yourself.

Three failures and a fire make a Scotsman's fortune.

Time tries a' as winter tries the kail.
Kail is said to be much improved once the first frosts have come, although this inevitably kills some of it off. Hence this proverb alludes to the idea that people who have suffered hardships in life can come through them much improved.

Tine needle, tine darg.
Literally this means that the person who loses their tools of the trade loses their day's work. A saying applied to lazy people who complain loudly when the first thing goes wrong with them.

To hain is to hae.
The motto of thrift.

To work for naething maks folk dead-sweer.
When there is no personal gain to be made, people are extremely averse to exertion.

Trot faither, trot mither; how can the foal amble?
You cannot escape your parentage easily.

Truth and honesty keep the crown o' the causey.
The crown o' the causey was the highest part of the street, which people kept to if they wanted to stay out of the mess in the gutter. Hence truth and honesty will keep one out of trouble.

Twa blacks winna make ae white.
Two wrongs do not make a right.

Twa heads are better than ane, though they're but sheep's anes.
Said when someone offers advice on a matter which you are considering.

Under water dearth, under snaw bread.
A flooded field will yield a poor crop, but one which has
been covered by the snow will flourish.

Unseen, unrued.
Out of sight, out of mind.

Untimeous spurring spoils the steed.

Upon my ain expense, as the man built the dyke.
A saying taken from the Kirkyard at Foot Dee or
'Fitty', in Aberdeen:
'I, John Moody, cives Aberdonensis,
Builded this kerk-yerd of fitty upon my own expenses.'

Use maks perfyteness.
Practice makes perfect.

Virtue is abune value.
There are certain things which cannot be bought.

Virtue ne'er grows auld.
Virtue is a quality which never ages.

Wad ye gar us trow that the mime's made o' green cheese, or that spade shafts bear plooms?
Would you really have us believe such an absurd tale?

Waes the wife that wants the tongue, but weels the man that gets her.
The wife who is quiet will have many troubles, but lucky is the man who marries her, i.e. silence is golden.

Waes unite faes.
Shared troubles can bring together one-time adversaries.

Wae to him that lippens to ithers for tippence.
Woe betide the person who trusts to another for a small obligation.

Waly, waly! bairns are bonny;
Ane's enough and twa's ower mony.
Potential parents beware!

Want o' wit is waur than want o' gear.

War's sweet to them that never tried it.
A warning to the young not to be taken in by the seeming glamour of war.

Wealth gars wit waver.
A warning of the power of money to make fools of us all.

Wealth has made mair men covetous than covetousness has made men wealthy.

We can shape their wylie coat, but no their weird.
We can influence somebody's appearance, but not their destiny.

Wedding and ill wintering tame baith man and beast.
A rather severe view of the 'hardship' of marriage.

Weel saipet is half shaven.
This saying, ascribed to Dr Hill of St Andrews, was his humorous Scottish translation of the old Latin aphorism *'Qui bene cepit dimidium facti fectit.'*

Weel won corn should be housed ere the morn.
'Weel won' corn meant that it had been dried by exposure to the air. This proverb urges people not to leave a job half done lest everything be lost.

Welcome's the best dish in the kitchen.
A testimony to the power of good hospitality.

We'll bear wi' the stink, when it brings in the clink.
So long as they are profitable, we will endure hardships.

We'll meet ere hills meet.
That is to say – never!

We'll ne'er big sandy bowrocks thegither.
We will never build sandcastles together, i.e. we will never be on intimate terms.

Wha comes oftener, and brings you less?
A humorous remark made to a frequent visitor.

Wha daur bell the cat?
A question supposedly asked by an experienced mouse when another suggested that they put a bell round the cat's neck, to warn of its approach. This saying is well known to students of Scottish history. At the time of James III, the Scottish nobles proposed to meet at Stirling and take Spence, the King's favourite, and hang him. However the worldly wise Lord Gray is said to have asked the above question. The Earl of Angus undertook the task, accomplished it, and thereafter was known as Archibald Bell-the-Cat.

What fizzes in the mou' winna fill the wame.
Outward appearances can be deceptive.

What makes you sae rumgunshach and me sae curcuddoch?
Why are you so rude and unpleasant to me when I am so friendly and anxious to please you?

What's in your wame's no in your testament.
Spoken to encourage someone to eat, i.e. if they eat all that is in front of them they cannot possibly leave it in their will.

What's nane o' my profit shall be nane o' my peril.
A refusal to run a risk if there is no share of the spoils.

What's yours is mine, what's mine's my ain.
Motto adopted by selfish partners.

What ye want up and doun you hae hither-and-yont.
Hither-and-yont means topsy turvy. A saying applied to someone who has all the necessary parts to complete a task, but not necessarily in the right place.

What ye win at that ye may lick aff a het girdle.
The prospect of success is exceedingly slim.

Whaur th' Tweed droons ane, the Till droons twa.
A warning to any traveller on approaching the banks of the latter river.

When all fruit fa's, welcome ha's.
Said when we start eating the coarser food when we have finished the finer fruits.

When Craigowl puts on his cowl, and Coolie Law his hood,
The folk o' Lundie may look dool, for the day'll no be good.
A piece of Angus weather lore, relating to the Sidlaw hills.

When Falkland Hill puts on his cap, the Howe o' Fife will get a drap,
And when the Bishop draws his cowl, look out for wind and weather foul!
Another piece of weather lore similar to the one above, but this time originating from Fife.

When I did weel I heard it never, when I did ill I heard it ever.
A reflection on the lack of positive reinforcement received. A saying applied to those who only give negative criticisms.

When my head's doun my house is theiked.
When I am busy I am free from debt.

When the Castle of Stirling gets a hat, the carse of Corntown pays for that.
When the clouds descend so low as to cover Stirling Castle, the surrounding environs may expect a deluge.

When the gudeman drinks to the gudewife a' wad be weel; when the gudewife drinks to the gudeman a's weel.
This saying suggests that in times past, a husband only drank to the good health of his wife through fear rather than affection.

When the hen gaes to the cock the birds may get a knock.
Spoken as a warning to the children of widows, i.e. when widows go looking for a second husband, the children may suffer as a consequence.

When the moon is on her back, Gae mend yer shoon and sort yer thack.
A piece of weather forecasting based upon the visible shape of the moon in the night's sky.

When the Yowes o' Gowrie come to land, The Day o' Judgement's near at hand.
Invergowrie is an ancient village and it claims to have had the first Christian church on the north side of the Tay. According to folklore, the Devil was so outraged by this act of defiance that he began throwing stones across the water at the new church. Two stones fell short and became known as the 'Goors, or Yowes, of Invergowrie'. A third stone overshot by half a mile and is now called the Deil's Stane. Hence the above prophetic rhyme which was supposedly recorded by Thomas the Rhymer.

When wine sinks, words soom.

When ye can suit your shanks to my shoon, ye may speak.
Don't speak about me until you have been in a similar situation yourself.

When ye Christen the bairn, ye should ken what to ca't.
Said to a vendor who is hesitant at giving the price of something.

Where MacGregor sits is head of the table.
Wherever the important person chooses to be is the centre of the action. This saying is sometimes attributed to Rob Roy MacGregor, the Highland outlaw. However the saying is used in many different lands where other names are substituted.

Whiles you and whiles me, sae gaes the bailierie.
A saying used when people get positions of authority in turns.

Wi' an empty hand nae man can hawks lure.
You cannot expect to attract workers unless you offer them something.

Wide lugs and a short tongue are best.
People who hear everything, but repeat none of it are safest.

Wide will wear but tight will tear.
Addressed to someone if they complain that an article of clothing is on the large side.

Woo sellers ken aye woo buyers.
It takes one to know one.

Wrang count is nae payment.

Ye are as lang in tuning your pipes as anither wad play a spring.
You take as long in preparing to do something as another would in performing it.

Ye breed o' our laird, ye'll no do right and ye'll tak nae wrang.
Used in the past by people who had suffered at the hands of the local master.

Ye breed o' Saughton swine, your nebs never out o' an ill turn.
Said of a troublemaker.

Ye breed o' the chapman, ye're never oot o' your gate.
A saying applied to those who do business wherever they go.

Ye breed o' the gowk, ye hae ne'er a rhyme but ane.
Used when someone always talks on the same subject.

Ye breed o' the tod, ye grow grey before ye grow gude.

Ye canna gather berries aff a whinbush.
Don't expect favours from ill-humoured people.

Ye canna get leave to thrive for thrang.
Literally, you are so busy you don't have time to get rich.

Ye canna mak a silk purse oot o' a sow's lug.

Ye canna preach oot o' your ain pu'pit.
A saying applied to people who are not very adept at describing things which do not usually occur in their everyday lives.

Ye come o' the M'Taks, but no o' the M'Gies.
Spoken of those more eager to receive than to give.

Ye crack crousely wi' your bannet on.
A not so subtle hint that a person is being over familiar.

Ye cut lang whangs aff ither folk's leather.
Said to cheeky people who are a little too free in their use of other's property.

You daur weel but ye downa.
You try to do well, but cannot.

You didna draw sae weel when my mear was in the mire.
You were not as helpful to me as I am being to you.

Ye fand it where the Hielandman fand the tangs.
You found it in its proper place. Used as a way of suggesting that someone has stolen something, when they say that they have just 'found' an object.

You fike it awa, like auld wives baking.
To 'fike' is to waste time in carrying out some business; to lose time by procrastination while appearing to be busy.

Ye hae a streak o' carl hemp in you.
You possess a strong will and mind. The carl hemp was the toughest fibre.

Ye hae been smelling the bung.
You've been drinking.

Ye hae come in time to tine a darg.
You have come in time to lose a day's work, i.e. you're too late.

Ye hae gien the wolf the wedders to keep.
You have entrusted a thing to someone who will either lose, spoil, or use it himself.

Ye hae gotten a ravelled hemp to redd.
You have got a very complicated situation to sort out.

Ye hae little need o' the Campsie wife's prayer, 'That she might aye be able to think enough o' hersel.'
Applied to conceited or selfish individuals.

Ye hae sew'd that seam wi' a het needle and a burning thread.
Said facetiously when a hasty repair gives way.

Ye hae the best end o' the string.
You have the best of the argument.

Ye hae tint the tongue o' the trump.
You have lost the main thing. A 'trump' is a Jew's Harp, and to lose the tongue of it is to lose what is essential to its sound.

Ye hae tint yer ain stamach an' found a tyke's.
A humorous saying applied to those who eat a great deal when they are hungry.

Ye'll get waur bodes ere Beltane.
Applied to someone who refuses the price offered for an object, suggesting that worse offers will be made before the 1st of May.

Ye'll hae the half o' the gate and a' the glaur.
You'll have half of the road and all of the mud. Said in jest when we make someone walk on the outside of a footpath.

Ye'll ne'er craw in my cavie.
You will never be welcomed into my house.

Ye'll never mak a mark in your Testament by that bargain.
You will probably lose money by that deal.

Ye'll neither dee for your wit nor be drown'd for a warlock.
A saying applied to those we consider to be lacking in both wisdom and intelligence.

Ye loe a' ye see, like Rab Roole when he's ree.
Spoken as a rebuke to greedy persons. When Rab Roole was 'ree' he was crazy with drink.

Ye look like Let-me-be.
You look very quiet and inoffensive.

Ye maun hae't baith simmered and wintered.
To 'simmer and winter' is to take a long time in thinking or formulating a plan.

Ye maun redd your ain ravelled clue.
You must sort out your own difficulties for yourself.

Ye may gang farther and fare waur.

Ye're a' blawin' like a burstin' haggis.
You are full of hot air.

Ye're a corbie messenger.
As with the raven sent out from Noah's ark, this saying is applied to those who are sent on an errand but who do not return.

Ye're an honest man, and I'm your Uncle – that's twa big lees.
Said to compulsive liars.

Ye're as stiff as a stappit faster.
You are full. A 'stappit faster' is a crammed pudding.

Ye're cawking the claith ere the wab be in the loom.
You are chalking the cloth before the yarn is in the loom. Another version of counting your chickens before they've hatched.

Ye're come o' blude, and sae's a pudding.
Said to deflate someone who is boasting of their noble lineage.

Ye're like an ill shilling – ye'll come back again.
A humorous saying applied to those who are about to depart.

Ye're like the miller's dog – ye lick your lips ere the pock be opened.
Said to greedy people who are ready to receive before they have even been offered something.

Ye rin for the spurtle when the pat's boiling ower.
You are too late in taking precautions.

Ye shape shune by your ain shauchled feet.
You judge others by your own poor standards.

Ye've grown proud since ye quatted the begging.
Said satirically to people who walk by without acknowledging one's acquaintance.

Ye wad do little for God an the deil was dead.
A sarcastic way of expressing one's doubt that a person
would be well behaved were it not for fear, rather than
because of the principle involved.

Ye wad wheedle a laverock frae the lift.
You would charm the birds from the sky.

Ye was ne'er born at that time o' year.
Said to people who expect a certain place or condition which
is considered above their birth.

Your een's greedier than your guts.
You want more than you can handle.

Your purse was steekit when that was paid for.
A manner of suggesting that the article in question has not
already been paid for.

**Yule is young on Yule even, and as auld as Saint
Steven.**

Glossary

A

a'	all
abune	above
adreich	askant, or at a distance
ae/ane	one
aff	off
afore	before
ahint	behind
ain	own
aith	oath, promise
aiver	a cart horse
ance	once
anither	another
auld	old
aumrie	cupboard
auncient	ancient
ava	at all
awa	away
aye	always

B

bairn(s)	child(ren)
baith	both
bannet	bonnet
bannocks	homemade flour cakes
barefit	barefoot

bauld	bold
bawbee	halfpenny
bawty	a dog
beild	shelter
beit	to renew, kindle
Beltane	the first of May
belyve	immediately, bye and bye
bicker	small wooden dish
bide	to stay
big	to build
biggin	a building, small house
bink	bench, seat
birk	birch
bit	piece
blate	bashful
blaw	to blow
bleer-e'ed	bleary eyed, or weak sighted
bode	a portent, or to earnestly wish for
bore	hole
bouk	bulk
bourd	a jest, to fool with
bowrock	a heap, a clump
brae	hillside, steep road
brak	to break
brat	a coarse apron
braw	fine
breed	to resemble, to take after
breeks	trousers
brither	brother
brose	a dish of oatmeal and water
browst	a brewing
browster	a brewer
brugh	the halo effect around the sun or moon
bubbly-jock	turkey cock
buirdly	strongly made, stout
bum	to buzz like a bee
buskit	dressed, decorated
but-and-ben	two adjoining rooms

C

ca'	to call, to name, to drive
cadger	beggar
carlin	old woman
cauff	chaf
cauld	cold
cawk	to chalk
chafts	chops
chancy	lucky, fortunate
chanter	the drone of a bagpipe
chapman	a pedlar
chiel	a young man, or a fellow
chokit	choked
claes	clothes
clink	money
clout	cloth
clung	empty
cog	wooden dish, milk pail
coo	cow
corbie	a raven
cottar	peasant labourer
counts	sums or accounts
cowp	to tip
cowte	colt
crab	to be angry
crack	to chat, a chat
craik	to complain
craw(ing)	to crow, crow(ing)
creep	to crawl
creeshy	oily, greasy
crooning	singing
crouse	bold, courageous
culye	to gain, to draw forth
curcuddoch	friendly, warm with affection

D

dae	to do
daffin'	playing
darg	a day's work
daur	to dare
daurna	dare not
daw	drab
dawly	untidy, slovenly
dawt	to dote on, to pet
deave	to deafen
dee	to die
deem	to judge
deil	devil
ding	to knock over, to surpass
dinna	do not
dint	chance
dit	to close
dizzen	dozen
dochter	daughter
doesna	does not
dominie	school master
donsy	unlucky, unfortunate
doo	dove, pigeon
dool	sorrow, misfortune
dosen	to settle/cool down
douce	repectable
draff	brewer's grain
drap	a drop, a small drink
dree	to endure, to suffer
drouth(y)	thirst(y)
dub	puddle
dune	done, exhausted

E

ee(n)	eye, eyes
e'ening	evening
eident	diligent
eider	more prominently
eild	age, old age
eird	earth
eith	easy
eme	uncle
ettle	to endeavour, to aim, an intention

F

fa'	fall
fain	eager, keen, anxious
fair fa'	good luck
faither	father
fand	found
farden	a farthing
fash	trouble
fashious	troublesome
fause	false
feckless	silly or weak (mentally or physically)
ferlie	to wonder at, a wonder
fit	foot, or to count up
fleech	to flatter
flesh-flee	bluebottle
fley	to frighten
flichter	flutter
fling	to kick, to jilt
flisket	fretful, easily annoyed or upset
flit	to move house
foisonless	insipid, without substance
forefoughten	fatigued
forejeskit	jaded, worn out
forejidged	prejudged

frae	from
fremit	strange
fu'	full
furdersome	industrious

G

gab	to speak, the mouth
gae	go
gaislin	gosling
gang	to go
gar	to force, to cause
gate, gait	road, way
gaunt	to yawn
gawsie	jolly, plump, handsome
gaylie	middling
gear	wealth, possessions
ghaist	ghost
gie	to give
giff-gaff	give and take
girdle	a circular iron plate used for baking
girnin'	fretful, grinning
glaiket	wanton, playful, trifling
glaur	mud, mire
glib	quick, ready in speech
gloom	frown
gowd	gold
gowk	a simpleton
gowpen	two hands joined together to contain something, or the quantity so contained
graip	dung fork
graith	harness
gramashes	gaiters
gree	to agree
greet	to cry
grip	to catch
grosset	gooseberry

grund	ground
gude	good

H

ha'	hall
hae	to have
hail	whole
hain	to save, to economise, to use sparingly
hame	home
handfu'	handful
hansel	a gratuity, a present
hantle	a number, a quantity
hap	chance
haud	to hold
heid	head
het	hot
heuk	hook
Hielandman	Highlander
himsel	himself
hirsel	flock
hutch	poor cottage

I

ilka	each, every
ither	other

J

jouk	to avoid a blow, to yield to circumstances
jundie	a passing blow or thrust

K

kailyard	kitchen garden
kame	to comb, a comb
kamester	a wool comber
kebbuck	a cheese
keckle	to cackle
ken	to know
kep	to catch
kirn	churn
kittle	ticklish, or difficult
kyte	the belly
kythe	to appear

L

lack	to depreciate, to slight
laigh	low
laith	slow, reluctant
lang	long
langsyne	long ago, old times
laverock	a lark
lawin'	reckoning in a public bar
leal	loyal, true, honest
leddy	lady
lee	to lie, a lie
leear	a liar
len'	lend, a loan
lichtit	alighted
lift	sky
lippen	to trust, to depend upon
loan	lane
lo'e	love
loup	to leap, to jump
lout	to submit to, to stoop to
lowe	a flame

lug(s)	ear(s)
lurden	a worthless fellow

M

madge-howlet	an owl
mailin'	farm
mair	more
mak	to make
malison	a curse
marrow	an equal, a match
maun	must
maunna	must not
mavis	a thrush
mayna	may not
mear	mare
mease	to appease
mends	amends
mense	manners, discretion
mensefu'	discreet, well-mannered
menseless	unmannerly, rude, ill-bred, forward
messan	a mongrel dog
midden	dung heap
mim	prim, demure
mint	endeavour
mislear'd	mischievous, wild
misterfu'	needy, begging
mither	mother
moistify	to moisten, to drink
mony	many
mool	to crumble; the earth of a grave
mouthfu'	mouthful
mow	a heap e.g. hay or wood
moyen	interest, influence
muckle	great, much
mune	moon

N

nae	no
naething	nothing
nane	none
neb	nose, point
ne'er	never
nieve	fist, hand
nitty-now	a lousy head

O

olite	active, nimble
oo	wool
oot	out
orts	that which is rejected or set aside
ower	over
owercome	a common or overused expression
oxter	armpit

P

parritch	porridge
Pasch	Easter
pat	pot
perfyteness	perfection
pike	to pick
plack	two bodles, or one third of an old English penny
ploom	plum
pock	a bag, sack
poortith	poverty
pow	head
pownie	pony
pree	to taste
preen	a pin

Q

quire	choir
quo/quoth	said

R

raggit	ragged
raip	rope
rattan	rat
redd	to put in order, to sort out
ree	tipsy, drunk
reek	smoke
reive	to rob, to steal
remede	remedy
riggin'	the ridge of a house
rin	to run
rippling-kame	a flax comb
rive	to tear, to rent asunder
routh	many, an abundance
row	to roll up
rumgunshach	rude, unkind
ruse	to praise

S

sae	so
sair	sore
sairy	poor
sap	sop
sark	shirt
sauch	willow
saucht	peace, ease
saut	salt
saw	a proverb, wise words
scabbit	scabby

sca'd	scabbed, scared
scart	scratch
sea-maw(s)	seagull(s)
shank(s)	leg(s)
shanna	shall not
shauchle	to shuffle, to walk lazily
shaup	husk
shool	shovel
shoon/shune	shoes
sib	akin, related
sic	such
sicker	sure, certain
siller	silver, money
simmer	summer
sindle	seldom
skaith	injury, harm
sliddry	slippery
sma'	small
smit	infect
smoor	to smother
snaw	snow
snite	to blow one's nose
sonsy	healthy, thriving, prosperous
soom	swim
sooth	true
soutar	shoemaker
spail	a chip of wood
speir	to enquire/ask
spring	a tune
spurtle	short stick for stirring porridge
stamack	stomach
stane	stone
stark	strong
steek	a stitch, or to close
stey	steep
stirk	a young cow or bull
stoor	dust
stot	young bull or ox
stoup	a jug with a handle

strae	straw
stravaig	to stroll about idly
sturt	rage
sune	soon
sweerd/sweird	unwilling, slow, lazy, indolent
syne	since, after then

T

tae	toe
taiken	token
tak	to take
tangs	tongs
taupie/tawpie	a foolish or idle woman
taury	tarry
tent	care
theek	to hatch
thegither	together
thoom	thumb
thrang	throng, busy
thraw	to form
tine	to lose
tinkler	tinker
tint	lost
tocher	dowry
tod	a fox
toom	empty
toun	town
tout	to blow a horn
trewed	trusted, believed
trow	to believe
tulzie	a quarrel
twa	two
twal	twelve
tyke	a clumsy person, a dog

U

unca'd	uncalled
unco	very, extremely, or strange and unknown

W

wab	web
wabster	webster, weaver
wad	would
wae	woe, sadness
wame	stomach
wark	work
warling	a worldling
warr	outrun
Wast	West
wat	wet
watna	know not
waukrife	wakeful
waur	worse
weel	well
weet	to wet
weird	destiny
wersh	tasteless, insipid
wha	who
whang	a large slice, a thong
whase	whose
whaup	a curlew
whaur	where
whilk	which
wi'	with
widdie	a rope, gallows
wight	courageous
windlin	a bottle of straw or hay
winna	will not
wispit	cleaned, swept

wizen	throat
woo'	wool
woodie	diminutive of wood
wrang	wrong
wyte	to blame, to find fault with

Bibliography

Anderson, M.L., (ed.) *James Carmichaell Collection of Proverbs in Scots*. Edinburgh 1957.

Balfour (ed.) *Ray's Complete Collection of English Proverbs*. Fifth Edition 1813.

Fergusson, D., *Scottish Proverbs*, gathered together by David Fergusson, sometime minister at Dunfermline, and put *ordine alphabetico* when he departed this life *anno* 1598. Edinburgh 1641.

Fergusson, D., *Fergusson's Scottish Proverbs from the Original Print of 1641 together with a larger Manuscript Collection of about the same period hitherto unpublished*, ed. E. Beveridge. Edinburgh 1924.

Henderson, A., *Scottish Proverbs*. Edinburgh 1832. (Contains introductory essay by William Motherwell).

Hislop, A., *The Proverbs of Scotland*. Collected and arranged, with notes, explanatory and illustrative and a glossary. Glasgow 1862.

Kelly, J., *A Complete Collection of Scottish Proverbs Explained and made Intelligible to the English Reader*. London 1721.

MacGregor, E., *Scots Proverbs and Rhymes*. Edinburgh 1983.

Ramsay, A., *A Collection of Scots Proverbs dedicated to the Tenantry of Scotland*. Edinburgh 1737.

Scottish Notes and Queries. Periodical. In particular December 1889 – February 1890. Aberdeen.

Stevenson, B., *Stevenson's Book of Proverbs, maxims and familiar phrases*. 1949.

Stirling, W., *The Proverbial Philosophy of Scotland: An address to the School of Arts*. Stirling and Edinburgh 1855.

Trench, R.C., *On the Lessons in Proverbs: Being the substance of Lectures delivered to Young Men's Societies at Portsmouth and elsewhere*. 3rd Revised Edition. London 1854.